POETRY COMPETITION
FOR 11-18 YEAR-OLDS

GW01418197

POP!
The Power Of Poetry

Surrey
Edited by Laura Martin

Young**Writers**

First published in Great Britain in 2006 by:
Young Writers
Remus House
Coltsfoot Drive
Peterborough
PE2 9JX
Telephone: 01733 890066
Website: www.youngwriters.co.uk

SB ISBN 1 84602 373 4

Foreword

This year, the Young Writers' *POP! - The Power Of Poetry* competition proudly presents a showcase of the best poetic talent selected from thousands of up-and-coming writers nationwide.

Young Writers was established in 1991 to promote the reading and writing of poetry within schools and to the young of today. Our books nurture and inspire confidence in the ability of young writers and provide a snapshot of poems written in schools and at home by budding poets of the future.

The thought, effort, imagination and hard work put into each poem impressed us all and the task of selecting poems was a difficult but nevertheless enjoyable experience.

We hope you are as pleased as we are with the final selection and that you and your family continue to be entertained with *POP! Surrey* for many years to come.

Contents

Josh Hughes (11)	38
Josie Whitman (11)	39
Catherine Daubney (12)	39
Charlie Payne (11)	40
Jessica Ferguson (11)	40
Albie Hitchcock (11)	41
Donna-Marie Keaton (12)	41
Emma Elliott (12)	42
Steven Jarman (12)	42
Joseph Wiltshire (12)	43
Jack Bates (11)	43
Hannah Everett (11)	44
Olivia Doble (11)	44
Hannah O'Connor (11)	45
Jake Cox (11)	45
Joseph Larter (12)	46
Lois Wood (11)	46
Callum Macarty (11)	47
Cerys Bristo (11)	47
Jordan Aldridge (11)	48
Rosie Weston (11)	48
Alice Green	49
Jack Bacon (11)	50
Laura Wood (11)	50

Coloma Convent Girls' School
Barbara Reddiar (14)	51

Coulsdon High School
Sam Hill (13)	52
Tanuja Singh (13)	52
Shanice Ryan (13)	53
Rochelle Faust (13)	53
Isla Perry (13)	54
James Regan (13)	54
Lauren Bailey (13)	55
Jack Ball (13)	55
Charmaine Prentice (13)	56
Ciara Williams	56
Louise Francis (13)	57
Holly Burraway (13)	57

James Francis (13)   58
Mason Weston (13)   58
Danielle Linnane (14)   59

Dunottar School
Jessica Bailey (14)   59
Lottie Husband (14)   60

Glyn Technology School
Thomas Penfare (13)   60
Ben Senneck (13)   61
James Penfare (13)   61
Cameron Maxton (12)   62

Nonsuch High School
Cathryn Antoniadis (12)   62
Alice Ahearn (12)   63
Kirsty Harrod (11)   64
Jennifer Williams (12)   65
Lydia Murtezaoglu (12)   66
Amy Tiri (13)   67
Lindsay Harrod (12)   68
Glynnis Morgan (14)   69
Serena Collins (14)   70
Hollie Irvin (11)   71

Philip Southcote School
John Hockley (14)   71
Christopher Buist (14)   72
Jai Patel (14)   72
Adam Leslie & Lee Stenning (14)   73
Ronnie Hughes, Michael Cole & Luis Pinto (14)   73
Kieron Carey (14)   74

Reigate Sixth Form College
Eleanor Luery (18)   74
Oliver Wright (16)   75
Red Saunders (16)   76
Rebecca Handcock (16)   77

Wallington County Grammar School

Sean Barry (11)	77
Fabio Carta (11)	78
Tom Harrison (12)	79
Sohail Khan (11)	80
Daniel Rodrigues (11)	80
Jaykishan Gudka (11)	81
Sam Nazarko (11)	81
Asher Carr (11)	82
Scott Fanner (12)	82
Thomas Tawse (12)	83
Alex Simpson (11)	83
Julian Chan-Diaz (11)	84
Sam Christy (12)	84
George McTaggart (11)	85
Allen Ola (12)	85
Nimesh Patel (11)	86
Gogulan Karunanithy (13)	87
Dilan Patel (11)	88
Sunmeet Kandhari (11)	89
Amos Pang (11)	90
Edmund Ryan (12)	90
Danyal Naseer (12)	91
Joseph Forrest (11)	91
Cameron Truscott (12)	92
Josh Bell (12)	93
Adam Asquith (12)	94
Adil Butt (13)	94
Oscar Ford (12)	95
Ben McLellan (12)	95
Joshua Castle (13)	96
Christopher Godwin (12)	97
Tom Housden (12)	98
Tom Wainford (13)	99
Nihar Majmudar (12)	100
Tom Kindler (13)	101
Michael Brockman (12)	102
Shatik Patel (12)	103
Salman Shahid (12)	104
Ryan Dansie (12)	105
Luke Davis (12)	106

The Poems

Life

People should not sink into any sort of bitterness,
The protective sun bursting, it's full of energy,
Power to destroy the terrorists' victory,
A citizen of the great, mighty, wise city of London,
Displaying patriotism,
Necessities in life,
Money, honour and reputation,

New beginnings,
Recovering from the 'Mayhem',
Made from old mistakes,
Destruction at the heart of London,
Devastating scenes of dreadful carnage,
Bodies torn,
Unthinkable images of suffering,
Same sacred feelings,
Many hearts full of hopes,
A few less aches,

Hidden messages,
Alive in people's memories
And untold lies,
Unfading memories,
And continuous sighs,

Dramatic changes are unforgettable,
Heartache and confusion,
Mixed with regret and tears,
Still living in adoration,
But never living the same fears.

Vajetha Nanthakumar (16)

Friends And Friendship

Friends and friendship
Richer than any rubies red,
Shining brighter than any star overhead,
Most valuable thing to Man that is known,
Is a true loving friend who lets you feel not alone.
This bond that two people share,
Of love, sacrifice and everlasting care,
Will last till the very end,
Because God chose him as my friend.
It is like a budding rose,
Day by day it strengthens and grows,
With a heart of gold that will never rust,
Because it is based on eternal trust.
Oh my friend, how shall I say,
Whether you are close or far away,
No distance can keep us apart,
As you are closest in my heart.
I'll listen to your thoughts and fears,
When you cry, I'll will wipe away the tears,
Like when needed, you were there,
Remember that I shall always be there,
You never know its value or cost,
Until it has somehow been lost,
Friends broke up in the past,
But I promise that I'll make this friendship last.
Moments and memories, good or bad,
Share we will, happy or sad,
Hand in hand through life we walk together,
For ever and ever and ever!
May this friendship between us always stay,
May God enable it to be that way!

Anas Ahmad Nasir (15)

Miss Midnight

Her skin was milky as an opal,
Her hair as black as a raven's feather,
Her eyes sparkled and twinkled bright,
As if they were imbedded with tiny stars.
Her fingers were long and pointed,
With rings made with gold and silver
Bejewelled with sapphire and onyx
Her lips were as red as blood,
Pursed, as if on the verge of speech,
As she gazed into space.
A clock chimed nearby,
It was time for her to make an entrance,
Miss Midnight was her name.

Caitlin Rozario (11)

Sam The Silver Dragon

My dragon has scaly skin,
He has a slippery, slimy tongue.
His silver body always slumps
Slumpishly on the sofa.
His name is Sam.
Sam's nose sits on his face
With slowly swinging snot.
Sam's eyes with silver pupils
Staring hungrily at the slithering snakes
Moving to safety.
Sam jumps up quickly for a snack.

Nicola Elliott (12)
Blenheim High School

I Love You McFly

Changing all the channels
Yeah, I'm bored like Hell
They made me switch it back
McFly should be in jail!
Their sound is just illegal
It's too good to be true
They rocked my world at once
And I don't know what to do.
Addicted to the tune
Five colours in her hair
I love the way they move
They make me stop and stare
They cast a spell on me
I love them way too much
I need to hear them loud
I need to feel their touch.
Whatever they are doing
It's working pretty well
I love you McFly
You totally rock my world!

Ellen Carthew (11)
Blenheim High School

My Dragon

My dragon breathes and bellows out
Fiery red flames
His enormous eyes and evil smile
Encourage people to see
His teeth are tremendous and terrible
And his loud nostrils are smelly nozzles
His wings are ginormous and his roar is incredible
His fierce growl is easy to hear
His mouth is gigantic and is full of saliva
My dragon is lovely to see.

Chloe Fox-Blach (11)
Blenheim High School

Red Dragon

My dragon belches boiling breath
Fierce fiery flames
Bold, blood-bursting skin
Massive mean monster
The dribbling dry dragon
Who can kill this scary killing thing?
Get it to go away
Be brave, be bold.
The nasty big nightmare
Fierce fiery flames.

Lauren Reed (11)
Blenheim High School

My Dragon, Dreadful

Dreadful's breath is blasting with blood
His enormous eyes are black and big
His teeth are tough and tremendous
And his scales are as hard as magic metal
Dreadful's wings are as large as the sun and Saturn
His claws are as sharp as slicing swords
He has the ears of a humungous horse
His heart is as horrible as a hummingbird.

Max Osborne (11)
Blenheim High School

August

It has a breeze like a fan on low
It has a sun like a bulb beaming brightly
It has clouds like fluffy wool
It has flowers popping up like party poppers.
It has water like a warm bath.

Sam Pengilly (11)
Blenheim High School

Guka
(Grandfather)

A man who struggled and fought for his life
Hero, a grandfather, a dad, someone to care
So many things to love in his noble life
A grandfather so special, a grandfather so rare.

Hero, a grandfather, a dad, someone to care
His kind gentle words that everyone hears
A grandfather so special, a grandfather so rare
And his last ever kind-hearted tears.

His kind gentle words that everyone hears
Sent to Heaven to live forever
And his last ever kind-hearted tears
We will never forget the man who brought us together
A man who struggled and fought for his life.

Sheila Karanja (11)
Blenheim High School

Hurricane Harry

Whizz! The hurricane appears
Whoosh! There goes my car.
The trees tremble to the ground,
The cows carry their calves away.
Superb shouts coming from the farmers,
Everything's moving away as fast as a cheetah running.
The path of the hurricane has left a long ditch in the ground.
There's destruction everywhere,
My hotel is ruined, falling to the ground like an exploding building.
Pigs are flying everywhere.
Who said pigs can't fly?

Harry Wales (11)
Blenheim High School

Christmas

Everyone's happy and smiling with glee
A day no one wants to pass
That's the way Christmas should be
This is the day we celebrate Christmas

The little ones put something out for Rudolph and Santa Claus
Whisky, milk, carrots and mince pies
They eagerly wait and then they pause
See them looking with staring eyes

You're opening your presents, one by one
In front of your family, oh what fun
By the time it's over, everything's done
Everyone's happy and no one's glum

Everyone's happy and smiling with glee
A day no one wants to pass
That's the way Christmas should be
This is the day we celebrate Christmas.

Ellen Frier (11)
Blenheim High School

The Thunderstorm

Knocking at the door violently, the crashing
thunderstorm bursts through,
Zapping everything in its path, the lightning
shines up the building.
Screaming children run away from the crazy enemy.
Eventually the storming rage of power drains
from the thunderstorm
And all is safe again, until it strikes again!

Marc Pryor (11)
Blenheim High School

The Day That Shook The Earth - Pantoum

The day that shook the Earth
For every country there's always a first
Throughout the earthquake there are births
Though this does not mean they are cursed!

For every country there's always a first
To be contained in one big quake
This does not mean they are cursed
This is the day the Earth will shake!

To be contained in one big quake
It is a horrific scene for those around
This is the day the Earth will shake
Huddling together without a sound!

It is a horrific scene for those around
Through an earthquake there are births
Huddling together without a sound
The day that shook the Earth!

Adam Brewer (11)
Blenheim High School

Snow

I will make children happy,
I will sing a jolly song,
I can lay a soft white blanket
But I can't stay long.

I will turn up and surprise you,
You can slip and slide on me,
But then I will go back to bed
And watch you from a tree.

Bethany Doyle (11)
Blenheim High School

My Amazing Dragon

My dragon darts and dodges
He heaves his heavy belly
And lets his flaming ferocious fire through
And eats like eight elephants, watching telly
He flies far, flapping frightfully
After every unfortunate incident
Like his lovely lovers, dying
He is still chirpy, cheerful and careful
So slimy snipers don't shoot him.
My dragon darts and dodges
And heaves his heavy belly.
Yet only I know about him
Because he's my invisible, imaginary, incredible friend!

Timothy Kendall (11)
Blenheim High School

Dragon Tim

Dragon Tim fires a ball of inferno flame,
Burning brightly at 1,000 degrees.
Tim's fiery breath gave him a name,
As cold turns to scorching every time he breathes.

His razor-like teeth also helped him,
As sharp as a thousand knives,
If you ever see Dragon Tim,
The teeth will give you the hives.

His claws clawed people to a terrible death,
Squeezing silently giving humans only a second of life,
Combined with an inferno breath
And with teeth like a knife.

He's unstoppable!

James Magraw (12)
Blenheim High School

Trees

They're big and tall
They're very shady
They're never small
Not thin like a lady

They're very shady
They have very thick bark
Not thin like a lady
They're in the park

They have very thick bark
You'd think nothing could hurt them
They're in the park
Till we chop down and burn them

You'd think nothing could hurt them
They're never small
Till we chop down and burn them
They're big and tall.

Amy Savage (11)
Blenheim High School

My Monster Poem

A head like a tomato,
A body like a small child.
Eyes like blue diamonds.
A nose like an elephant's nostril.
A snout like a giant parrot.
Teeth like a monkey.
Ears like a rabbit's.
Whiskers like a cat's.
A tongue like a big fat sausage.
Legs like a snail's tail.
Paws like a hazelnut.
Toes like a massive submarine.
Claws like a vampire's fangs.

Laura Gow (11)
Blenheim High School

Autumn - Pantoum

When all the leaves are falling
Everything is red and yellow
When the wind is calling
All things so mellow

Everything is red and yellow
Leaving its contents all over the place
All things so mellow
Leaves all over the wide open spaces

Leaving its contents all over the place
Everywhere you look colours
Leaves all over the wide open space
Everyone being smilers

Everywhere you look colours
When the wind is calling
Everyone being smilers
When all the leaves are falling.

Rosemary Samuels (11)
Blenheim High School

Hot-Breathing Dragon

My hot-breathing dragon,
Breathes burning fire
He is a blood-burning monster

His eyes look lovingly at his prey
He lounges about waiting
For his prey to approach him
Nobody can defeat this ten foot dragon.

Everyone is scared stiff of my dragon
That is my hot-breathing dragon
So be aware because he might turn on you!

Charlotte Davis (11)
Blenheim High School

Pantoum

This was the day the earthquake struck
40,000 people died
Nobody in Pakistan was in luck
Most people were homeless everybody said goodbye

40,000 people died
Every earthquake has a burp
Most people homeless, everybody said goodbye
Loads of people dying of thirst

Every earthquake has a burp
Every country has their first
Loads of people dying of thirst
It is now getting cold (need warmth)

Every country has their first
Nobody in Pakistan was in luck
It is now getting cold (need warmth)
This is the day the earthquake struck.

Connor Bliss (11)
Blenheim High School

The Tidal Wave

It gushed up the stairs and burst open the door of the library.
It slammed down on people, spinning them round and round.
It swirled thousands of books up and down,
crashing and crunching down on shelves.
It fell down like a plane crashing to the ground.
It was one big mess filling up to the top of the high glass ceiling.
It was as high as the Empire State Building.
It was truly, terrifyingly terrible and it lasted for ten terrifying hours,
until the clashing and crashing stopped and slowly started to
drain away.

Tom Welford (11)
Blenheim High School

Christmas

Christmas is a time for fun,
You get lots of presents and eat lots of food,
It's in the season where we don't see much sun,
People are in a very happy mood.

You get lots of presents and eat lots of food,
Silly socks and a silly laughing thing.
People are in a very happy mood,
Father Christmas likes to hear you sing.

Silly socks and a silly laughing thing,
Sparkling lights and pretty balls,
Father Christmas likes to hear you sing,
Glittery things fill the halls.

Sparkling lights and pretty balls,
Little hand that's freezing cold,
Glittery things fill all the halls,
For the old.

Reece Cope (12)
Blenheim High School

The Devious Dragon

His eyes are angry and almond-shaped
His treacherous teeth twinkle against the sparkling sun.

His mouth gives out glowing fire as bright as the sun.
His wings powerfully bellow blowing breeze as cold as ice.

His scales shine like the sun as the reflection from fire
flows from his mouth.

His legs lounge as he stares and looks longingly into space.
His heart booms as he lazily lies sleeping slowly.

Lucie Benson (12)
Blenheim High School

Pantoum About My Rabbit

My rabbit is a pest
He is big, he is round and he is cool
He always does his best
But he never goes to school

He is big, he is round, he is cool
He sits on his bum all day
But he never goes to school
And he always gets his way

He sits on his bum all day
He is very jumpy
And he always gets his own way
But he is very, very lumpy

He is very jumpy
He always does his best
But he is very, very lumpy
My rabbit is a pest.

Zoe Merrett (11)
Blenheim High School

Dare Dragon

My dragon is the meanest
His teeth are terrible and tiny
His fire fierce with flying flames
His tail as twisted as a tongue twister
My dragon's spine is as spiky as a spear
My dragon's wings are as wacky as a wild werewolf.
This is my dragon, don't dare mess with him!

Zoë Cudmore (11)
Blenheim High School

The Unicorn - Pantoum

The mystical, enchanted unicorn
Lighting up the winter forest
Using the magic of his horn
As the creatures of the day take to their nests.

Lighting up the winter forest
Bright and beautiful standing he
As the creatures of the day take to their nests
Most of those live in the tree.

Bright and beautiful standing he
The screeching animals scream out loud
Most of those live in the trees
There's the unicorn standing proud

The screeching animals scream out loud
Using the magic of his horns
There's the unicorn standing proud
The mystical, enchanted unicorn.

James Robert Cook (11)
Blenheim High School

My Fierce Dragon

My dragon breathes out fire,
Burning bellows and sparks.

His claws are like swords, big and sharp,
His eyes are big and fierce like fire.

His teeth are massive, as sharp as knives
His noisy nostrils are nozzles,
Throwing fierce, ferocious, burning sparks and flames.

Chelsey Boyd (11)
Blenheim High School

The Deadly Dragon

My dragon dangerously dug with its claws,
Breath bellowing fiery flames,
Ferociously writhing flicking eyes,
The piercing, tightly packed, prickly teeth,
Wings beating down bellowing boiling flames,
Thunderous feet thumping restlessly,
Rickety spines specked with blood,
The massive body backed with flame,
The sweeping tail swishes through the air,
The deadly dragon comes in for the strike.

Andrew Valentine (12)
Blenheim High School

My Dragon Spooks Everyone Out

My dragon fires fast out of his nose
My dragon stamps down the streets
Spitting and dribbling on people's slow legs.
My dragon has got googly eyes,
My dragon is the kindest dragon in the whole world,
He's the best.
My dragon has lovely eyes, you can't get your eyes off his.

Mary Louise Linda Palmer (11)
Blenheim High School

The Bellowing Dragon

His breath bellowed at bellowing speed,
His gigantic scorching eyes stared
Terrible and terrifying teeth
His noisy nose booming as he breathed.

Sophie Snowden (12)
Blenheim High School

A Dangerous Dragon

My dragon dangerously does dangerous things
He breathes and belches
His eyes are enormous and can be seen for miles around
His teeth never tremble, always terrible
His foolish face is never white with fear
His long legs, crawling with spiders
His fearsome fire burns frightened trees
His windy wings are so powerful
If only he could hear me!

Dominic Moore (12)
Blenheim High School

My Cousin Ella

She's a soft small pillow,
A perfect pink pansy, dancing in the wind.
She' a colourful rainbow filling the sky,
She's a bumblebee, flying from flower to flower,
The first drop of snow, delicate and precious,
A fairy-tale princess, kind and beautiful.
She's a sherbet lemon, strong and sweet,
She's summer, spring, autumn and winter.

Alice Fitzgerald (11)
Blenheim High School

My Dragon, Dolly

Her nails are marvellous and manicured,
Her hair is straightened so smooth.
Her eyes are blue and bold, but red when in a mood.
Her teeth are white and wonderful,
Her clothes are pretty, plus pink.
Her style so girly and glamorous,
All thanks to me!

Lucy Carrell (11)
Blenheim High School

The Fire-Breathing Dragon

My dragon has slimy skin
He has a slimy sticky tongue
He has a sweeping tail
He has razor-sharp teeth
He has googly eyes
He has a snotty nose
He has wings like fans
He has legs like tree stumps
He has a burning blast of fire balls
And he has a mouth as wide as a crocodile.

Daniel James (11)
Blenheim High School

My Friend

She's got a pair of legs that look like sausages,
She's got a face like an egg,
She's got hair like straw,
She's got ears as big as elephants.
She's got two eyes that look like two potatoes,
She's got arms that look like sticks,
And worst of all, she's a pig on stilts!

Tiffany Sykes (11)
Blenheim High School

Happy Hallowe'en

Happy Hallowe'en, kids constantly seeking candy,
Wicked witches, devious devils, vicious vampires,
Picturesque pumpkins, divine decorations, orange and black.
Sugar sweets and dinging doorbells,
Mean monsters and goofy ghouls and ghastly ghosts,
Laughter fills the land.

Brooke Fitzpatrick (11)
Blenheim High School

The World

The moon is bright
The sun is hot
The day is light
I drink a lot.

The sun is hot
Water is cool
I drink a lot
It's a good time to go to school.

Water is cool
I love dogs
It's a good time to go to school
In the fog.

I love dogs
The day is light
In the fog
The moon is bright.

Jamie Satchelle (11)
Blenheim High School

What Will Happen?

What will happen in the year 3002?
Nobody knows
I wish I knew
Will there be aliens do you suppose?
Will we find life on Mars?

Will there be cars?
Will humans be history?
I wish I knew
It's certainly a mystery.

Will humans be history?
I wish I knew
It's certainly a mystery
What will happen in the year 3002?

Charlotte Reid (11)
Blenheim High School

Hurricane - Pantoum

It killed millions
And broke their hearts
It seems like billions
They have fallen apart

And broken their hearts
They will all die
They have fallen apart
You can't get over it because they'll always cry

They will all die
Most of them don't care
You can't get over it because they'll always cry
It's so unfair

Most of them don't care
It seems like billions
It's so unfair
It killed millions.

George Hibberd (11)
Blenheim High School

My Dad

I sit in the chair and watch him
I remember when I was little
Walking along with him
And trying to do the same footsteps as him.
Trying to join in his conversations
Trying to be as important as him
Remembering how he's always
Made me feel safe and protected.
Sometimes now I don't know much about him.
Now he's older and frailer
But he's still my hero, he's my dad.

Annabella Morris (11)
Blenheim High School

The Moon!

Do you look up at the moon at night?
How it shines up high in its beauty.
Oh how it sits up there, oh so bright,
It sits there on duty.

How it shines up high in its beauty,
They all say there's a man on the moon.
It sits there on duty,
My dad says he will find out soon.

They all say there's a man on the moon,
When it's dark he comes out,
My dad says he will find out soon,
'It's so gorgeous,' I almost have to shout.

When it's dark, he comes out,
Oh how it sits up there, oh so bright,
'It's so gorgeous,' I almost want to shout,
Do you look up at the moon at night?

Taylor Rands (11)
Blenheim High School

Hurricane Orlando

Boom! Skyscrapers crashing down like 40 buses,
One on top of each other.
Swoosh! Preposterous winds, everything in their way.
Lightning is the legs of angry gods, treading air.
Rain is like monsoons, flooding cities in the world.
Dust and soot plummeting down streets
Like stampedes of furious rhinos.
It sounds like every member of the cat family growling
To show their hunger!
Hurricane Orlando
Going, going, gone.

Charlie Edwards (11)
Blenheim High School

Hallowe'en

Hallowe'en is a very scary time
We're going trick or treating
We're all looking grimy
Getting lots of sweets.

We're going trick or treating
Going to the dentist
Getting lots of sweets
There is lots of fog and mist.

Going to the dentist
Dressing up as 'Scream'
There is lots of fog and mist
Someone gave me whipped cream

Dressing up as 'Scream'
We're all looking grimy
Someone gave me whipped cream
Hallowe'en is a very scary time.

James Matthews (11)
Blenheim High School

My Mum

My mum's eyes look like cream pies,
her head looks like a Cadbury creme egg,
her nose looks like a double-sized ruler,
her mouth looks like an earthquake waiting to happen,
her body looks like a stick,
her knees look like wriggling worms,
her hair looks like a mad scientist that's
just had an explosion,
her feet smell like rotten eggs,
her ears look like a pointy pencil,
her teeth look like the sun on a bad day,
her chin looks like a pig's tail.
Now that concludes my mum.

Danielle Mais (11)
Blenheim High School

Earthquake - Pantoum

The terrible earthquake that struck
40 thousand die
All those people with bad, bad luck,
That's no lie.

40 thousand die,
Most are homeless
That's no lie.
Whoever survives, live their lives in a mess.

Most are homeless,
They need water.
Whoever survives live their lives in a mess.
All around is devastation and slaughter.

They need water,
All those people with bad, bad luck.
All around is devastation and slaughter,
The earthquake that struck.

Richard Teare (11)
Blenheim High School

My Brother

My brother is an ant
He is a master genius ant.
He is a little wooden stool, sat by the fire.
He is a bluebell, ringing at me.
He is the depths of winter, cold and inside.
He is mid-December, always wanting more.
He is a calm little Rover, dawdling along the road.
He is a shrunken pair of jeans,
Having been washed a thousand times.
He is a tiny pea, on an oversized plate.
He is an inch of lemonade left at the bottom of the glass.
He is a rainy day, but full of excitement.
He is Douglas Adams, thinking the impossible.
This is my brother.

Philippa Ridgway (11)
Blenheim High School

My Little Next Door Neighbour

My little next door neighbour has sweet little glistening diamond eyes,
Her little nose is a tiny button.
Her little mouth is 4cm with lips as red as the reddest rose.
Her short hair is short, from her face to her chin
And gold as the new one pound coin.
She is as short as a metre stick, maybe a bit bigger.
Everything about her is so sweet, she's a glistening diamond to me.

Sarah Louise Ribalta (11)
Blenheim High School

Christmas

Snow underfoot like honeycomb crushed up,
Mistletoe hanging around the house like bats,
Baubles hanging on the tree like round boiled sweets,
Crackers *bang, pop, whizz*, like fireworks shooting around,
Lights flashing and changing, like traffic lights,
Santa, big, fat and cuddly, like a squishy teddy bear,
Reindeer with bells gallop through the air, like bells in a band,
Snowmen stand still and watch, like a guard.

Michaela Pettit (11)
Blenheim High School

It's Christmas Time!

It needs . . .
Glittering baubles like twinkling stars on a moonlit night,
Flying reindeer like a bird flying in the sky,
A robin sitting on a snowy branch like a monkey swinging from one,
A big jolly man like Santa, sorting out who's been naughty or nice.
Parents raiding the shops for presents, like a stampede of elephants.
A choir singing like a band at a concert.
This is Christmas!

Lauren McVeigh (11)
Blenheim High School

Hallowe'en

Ghosts and witches are believed to appear,
Pumpkins and witches are full of sweets,
Be careful, slayers might carry a spear,
Monsters come at your door shouting trick or treat.

Pumpkins and witches full of sweets,
Ghosts wear white,
Monsters come at your door shouting trick or treat,
Devils feel tight.

Ghosts wear white,
Children dress up to go to the party,
Devils feel tight,
At the end of the party you might get a Smartie.

Children dress up to go to the party,
Be careful, slayers might carry a spear,
At the end of the day you might get a spear,
Ghosts and witches are believed to appear.

Gursharan Dhillon (12)
Blenheim High School

Christmas

Christmas needs . .
A sparkly tree twinkling bright.
A furry hat, warm and cosy.
Lots of presents to bring people together.
Some bubbly drink fizzing like a bubble bath.
Some festive lights like Rudolph's nose.
Thick snow layered on the ground like a woolly blanket.
Red and green Christmas crackers banging as loud as a lion's roar.
Baubles hanging on the tree, twinkling like a baby's playpen.
Mistletoe hanging high above the love.
This is what happens on Christmas Day.

Hayley Grimwood (11)
Blenheim High School

Where I Go Skiing

Where I go skiing
There's always lots of snow
Down slopes I go whizzing
But then I never know where to go.

There's always lots of snow
Right up to your knees
But then I never know where to go
Because it's so cold there's never any bees.

Right up to your knees
The snow is falling down
Because it's so cold there's never any bees
Right down to the ground.

The snow is falling down
Down slopes I go whizzing
Right down to the ground
Where I go skiing.

Lauren Wilkes (11)
Blenheim High School

Football

Hat-trick hero,
Three goals to zero.
Cup Final winner,
Excellent winger.
Free kick taker,
Skilful playmaker.
Tackling defender,
Injury mender.
Attackers scoring,
The game is not boring.

Scott Brown (11)
Blenheim High School

The Dreaded Thing!

The dreaded thing has nearly reached my den,
It's been seen by many men,
It also frightens me, a child
As I know it is wild.
It is clear that it has returned again.

We children were told to stay in bed,
To keep our pillows over our head.
'You don't need to panic,'
Claimed a friendly mechanic,
'It will go away,' he said.

But I couldn't take not knowing what it was anymore,
In my mind I had to be sure.
So I went down to the moor
Where it had been spotted before,
And I got chased by an angry boar.

When it lost me, I hid by a tree,
Wondering what did it want with me?
Then I heard something burp
And it said with a slurp,
'You're going to be very tasty!'

'I'm sorry, it was a mistake coming here,
You can see I'm full of fear!'
It scratched its head
But then just said,
'I'm still going to eat you,' it said.

I quickly escaped and decided to leave it in peace,
So I went home in disbelief,
It must have been a dream,
But then I heard a scream
And I saw its paw print on a leaf!

Hannah Jones (11)
Blenheim High School

A Cat's Life

Cute and cuddly kitty cat,
Sitting in the sun,
Cute and cuddly kitty cat,
Having so much fun.

Cute and cuddly kitty cat,
Wash your little head,
Cute and cuddly kitty cat,
Go upstairs to bed.

Cute and cuddly kitty cat,
Chase the butterflies,
Cute and cuddly kitty cat,
You've got lovely eyes.

Cute and cuddly kitty cat,
Purr your little song,
Cute and cuddly kitty cat,
You're my little Tom.

Cute and cuddle kitty cat,
Scrambling round the house,
Cute and cuddly kitty cat,
Chase that crazy mouse.

Cute and cuddly kitty cat,
Love you to the core,
Cute and cuddly kitty cat,
Love you for evermore.

Helena Fox (12)
Blenheim High School

Mum

She is a soft dolphin
She is a pink limo
She is a quiet song
She is a cheese pizza
She is also a red rose.

Patricia DeSousa
Blenheim High School

My Monster Poem

My monster has a . . .

A head like an oversized fist.
A body like a brown chocolate bar.
Ears like panting seal flippers.
A nose like a crocodile snout.
Claws as sharp as Godzilla's.
Eyes like creamy custard pies.
Wings like a golden eagle's.
A tail like a slithering snake.
A tongue like a giraffe's.
Teeth like sharp arrow points.
Scales as hard as iron.
Arms as muscly as the strongest man.
Paws like sharp daggers piercing.
Flaps of skin between the toes and paws.

Michael Riches (12)
Blenheim High School

The Guy That Travelled The World

The guy that travelled the world is a funny thing.

He's got a head, like a Norwegian boat,
Hair like the Pacific Ocean,
Eyes shaped like Ayers Rock,
Nose that goes down like Niagara Falls,
His large mouth as big as the Empire State Building,
Teeth like Big Ben,
Voice (I don't want to tell you) as loud as St Paul's!
Ears as big as the Eiffel Tower,
Legs as tall as the Leaning Tower of Pisa,
Feet are large (really x 100) as big as the Parthanon!

So this is the guy that travelled the world . . .
I don't know him.

Ben Slade (11)
Blenheim High School

Those Unfortunate

Think about those unfortunate
All those have been ruined by the weather
Now children have grown unfit
No food, no weight, just like a feather

All those have been ruined by the weather
Everything lost, all destroyed
No food, no weight, just like a feather
Now they are left to get annoyed

Everything lost, all destroyed
Houses gone, shattered to pieces
Now they are left to get annoyed
40,000 died, uncles, aunties and nieces

Houses gone, all shattered to pieces
Now children have grown unfit
40,000 died, uncles, aunties and nieces
Think about those unfortunate.

Emma Titchener (11)
Blenheim High School

Monster Madness!

It needs . . .
A head like the top of the Millennium Dome.
A body the size of Blenheim High School.
Eyes like sweet custard pies,
Claws as sharp as swords.
A nose as big as a football,
Hands as big as humans.
Legs like the Eiffel Tower.
Ears the size of tanks,
Arms as long as bamboo sticks.

Luke Pudar (11)
Blenheim High School

Summer

Summer is the best time of the year
People are on their holidays
Everyone is on the pier
You should leave on Sunday.

People are on their holidays
There are children swimming in the sea
You should leave on Sunday
The best on the beach is definitely me.

There are children swimming in the sea
People are sunbathing on the sand
The best on the beach is definitely me
If you don't like summer I don't understand.

People are sunbathing on the sand
Everyone is on the pier
If you don't like summer I don't understand
Summer is the best time of the year.

Georgia Cohen (11)
Blenheim High School

Christmas

It needs . . .
A tree as big as a rocket.
Decorations like sparkling diamonds.
Snowflakes falling like beautiful pearls.
Christmas crackers, as loud as exploding fireworks.
Santa is coming in his big red sleigh
Like an enormous flying car.
And lots of presents like a new big toy shop.

Hannah Pinto (11)
Blenheim High School

The Simpsons - Pantoum

I like The Simpsons
Their skin is bright and it has a glow.
I like them more than Lintons
I even like watching it in the snow.

Their skin is bright and has a glow.
Mr Burns is skinny and old.
I even like watching it in the snow.
My favourite character's Homer, who's bald.

Mr Burns is skinny and old,
He once ran over Bart.
My favourite character's Homer who's bald.
I wish The Simpsons didn't part.

He once ran over Bart,
I like them more than Lintons.
I wish The Simpsons didn't part.
I like The Simpsons.

Luke Conroy (11)
Blenheim High School

Christmas

It needs . . .
A tree as big as a mountain
Lights as bright as the sun
Santa as big as an elephant
Nose as red as Rudolph
Freezing cold, as cold as snowmen
Crackers as loud as a stampede
Stockings as long as a giraffe's neck.

Sarah Pragnell (11)
Blenheim High School

Tornadoes

The spin of a tornado is twirling.
It makes a terrible noise.
It moves about and it is curling.
It sucks up the moist.

It makes a terrible noise.
All of the lights go out.
It sucks up the moist.
No more people go out or about.

All of the lights go out.
All the cars are flying up.
No more people go out or about.
There are things flying like cups.

All the cars are flying up.
It moves about and it is curling.
There are things flying like cups.
It sucks up the moist.

Nathan Mannion (12)
Blenheim High School

My Grandad

My grandad is a lively five-year-old,
He is the warm month of July.
He is a tall oak tree,
He is a lightning fast Ferrari,
He is a glowing sunshine,
He is the lovely season of summer,
He is a laughing hyena,
That's my grandad.

Alex Gardiner (11)
Blenheim High School

The Winter

Winter is the season of snow
Snowballs being thrown around
In the winter Santa goes ho ho ho!
Snow falls down to the ground.

Snowmen with a carroty nose
Snowballs going up and down
As the children played the snow rose
The snow keeps going round and round.

Soon the sun comes out, the snowman melts
All the snow goes away
Then the rain pelts
The snow goes away for another day.

Winter is the season of snow
Snowballs being thrown around
In the winter Santa goes 'Ho, ho, ho!'
Snow falls down to the ground.

Sam Christmas (11)
Blenheim High School

On The Move

When a bat flies, it flaps,
When an elephant moves, it stamps.
When birds are about to fly, they sigh,
When lions have enough of our talk, they walk.
When kangaroos jump, they stamp,
When monkeys are in the trees, they flow in the breeze.
When penguins waddle, they dawdle.
When lions are about to bite, they turn all white.

Huw Morgan (11)
Blenheim High School

My Favourite Month - Pantoum

My favourite month is June,
There is so much to do,
Because there is always a full moon,
And I make people frightened by shouting boo!

There is so much to do,
I like swimming in my luxurious pool
And I make people frightened by shouting boo
And I make myself cool.

I like swimming in my luxurious pool,
Playing with my friends is fun
And I make myself cool,
I especially like to eat hot cross buns.

Playing with my friends is so much fun,
There is always a full moon,
I especially like to eat hot cross buns,
My favourite month is June.

Angus Stewart (11)
Blenheim High School

My Friend Lauren Wiggins

She is a bright sunshine
A new Mariah Carey
A funny joker
A lively puppy
A sweet jar of honey
A colourful butterfly
A bright sunflower
A bouncy ball
And that's why she's my friend Lauren.

Olivia Hitchcock (11)
Blenheim High School

The World

As the tree begins to die
Everything goes black
As the world passes by
I can feel my world crack.

Everything goes black
As the world crashes around our ears
I can feel my world crack
After all these years.

As the world crashes around our ears
I begin to cry
After all these years
I really need to try.

I begin to cry
As the world passes by
I really need to try
As the tree begins to die.

Alice Bickerstaff (11)
Blenheim High School

My Autumn Poem

Friends fire fireworks and they fly
far into the moonlit sky.
Everyone shouts and screams,
as the stars twinkle and gleam.

Leaves lower down,
deep to the lovely ground.
They twist and turn,
tumble and churn into the twilight sky.

Chandni Modha (11)
Blenheim High School

Summer - Pantoum

Summer is hot,
The sun is all over the place,
You hear the horses trot
And you get a bright red face.

The sun is all over the place,
I like playing in the pool,
You get a bright red face,
Everyone's looking really cool.

I like playing in the pool,
I go to the beach,
Everyone's looking really cool,
The lucky teachers don't have to teach.

I go to the beach,
You hear the horses trot,
The lucky teachers don't have to teach,
Summer is hot.

Libby Mulqueen (11)
Blenheim High School

I'd Rather . . .

I'd rather be a bird than a pig,
I'd rather wear a hat than a wig.

I'd rather have a mansion than a house,
I'd rather be a lion than a mouse.

I'd rather have some chocolate than a carrot,
I'd rather be a sheep than a parrot.

I'd rather have lemonade than coke,
I'd rather kick than poke.

I'd rather be young than old,
I'd rather be bought than sold.

Rebecca Cotton (11)
Blenheim High School

Christmas

Christmas is like a basket of joy with snow
like frothy milk on top of a cappuccino.
A robin is like the blue tit of winter
its chest smothered in fresh summer cherries.
Presents are like little boxes of dreams.
A decorated Christmas tree is like a mountain of jewels,
each jewel unique and special in its own special way.
Santa is the king of wishes but never has been seen,
he only appears when we're fast asleep enjoying a dream.

Alexander Millroy (12)
Blenheim High School

December

The snow is white candyfloss being played with it
The ice is like icing sugar with a shell
The presents like different-shaped boxes covered in wrapping paper
The Christmas tree with amazing decorations and a star at the top
The cold as a freezer sitting in the garage outside
The gloves, hat and scarf keep you as warm as the sun
Snowmen like three different sizes of ice cream
The snowball like a white bouncy ball.

Harriet Pinch (11)
Blenheim High School

Hurricane

Twirling, whirling, crashing down
On Blenheim High but mainly the town.
On the houses like Bob the Builder's hammer
This wasn't in the mayor's daily planner.
Stopped suddenly, silence.

Josh Hughes (11)
Blenheim High School

My Friends - Pantoum

Friends are very important to me
They're fun, friendly, sensible and kind
They're everything I want them to be
But some are very hard to find.

They're fun, friendly, sensible and kind
Me and my friends meet at school
But some are very hard to find
After school we meet in the mall.

Me and my friends meet at school
At the weekends we go to the park
After school we meet in the mall
Then we go off to Mark's.

At the weekends we go to the park
They're everything I want them to be
Then we go off to Mark's
Friends are very important to me.

Josie Whitman (11)
Blenheim High School

My Cousin

She is the cool leather sofa
Overflowing with white Louis Vuitton cushions
She is the Burberry carpets
Running throughout Paris Hilton's luxury pad.
She is the shiny gold round my Next necklace
With 'to die for' diamanté engravings.
She is the loud, wacky party going on
Until the early hours of the morning.
She is the sweetest chocolate,
That makes your mouth water.
But she is the best, wickedest cousin
Anyone could wish for!

Catherine Daubney (12)
Blenheim High School

The Horrible Dog I Know

I know a dog who never barks
He's lazy, boring and not very fun
But he likes to go to parks
And likes to lay all day in the sun.

He's lazy, boring and not very fun
He likes to eat so much food
And likes to lay all day in the sun
And he's always in a mood.

He likes to eat so much food
His fur is mucky and wet
And he's always in a mood
He's not my favourite pet.

His fur is mucky and wet
But he likes to go to parks
He is not my favourite pet
I know a dog who never barks.

Charlie Payne (11)
Blenheim High School

Who Is This?

She is as beautiful as a butterfly,
She is like a queen on a chair,
Her hair is like a warm cushion,
She is as sweet as a strawberry,
She is as nice as a cola bottle sweet,
She is as loud as an elephant,
She is as bouncy as a kangaroo,
She is louder than anyone I know,
But most of all she is my best friend.

Jessica Ferguson (11)
Blenheim High School

Football

The crowds are always screaming.
The footballers are playing.
The floodlights are beaming.
The managers are obeying.

The FA Cup is the best cup.
Chelsea brought the league.
Every team wants to lift the FA Cup.
It's every team's dream.

Ronaldinho is the best player in the world.
Papa Diop has a hard shot.
All Beckham's shots have curled.
The players hate it when it's hot.

You have to work hard in training.
Every Premiership player gets paid over £1,000
But every player will be complaining.
Every Premiership football ground has a capacity over 10,000.

Albie Hitchcock (11)
Blenheim High School

Shall I Compare You To My Cat Malteser?

You are more cool than a green cucumber
and prettier than a rose,
you are funnier than a clown,
you are soft and slip all the time like snow.

You are more calm than a wavy, calm sea
and I am glad you will be with me.

You make me feel happy and jolly,
when I don't see you I miss you lots,
I love it when you stay with me
and when me and you get an ice lolly.

Donna-Marie Keaton (12)
Blenheim High School

Chocolate

Some chocolate's bubbly,
Some chocolate's smooth,
Some makes me feel warm and cuddly,
Some makes me want to dance and move.

Some chocolate's smooth,
Some chocolate's crunchy,
Some makes me want to dance and move,
I like to eat a Munchie.

Some chocolate's crunchy,
There's different chocolate such as dark, milk and white,
I like to eat a Munchie,
It's so tasty I couldn't put up a fight.

There's different chocolate such as dark, milk and white,
Some makes me feel warm and cuddly,
It's so tasty I could put up a fight,
Some chocolate's bubbly!

Emma Elliott (12)
Blenheim High School

The Tremendous Thunder

The tremendous thumping thunder flew through the grass,
smashing down the roofs of the Year 7 class.
It flashed with a bang, as trees started to hang,
that's when the bells and the phones rang.
It then crashed down the trees, and didn't know what to do,
so I sat in the cupboard shaking on my knees.
Wildly it dashed, through the air
and I flipped off my chair.

Steven Jarman (12)
Blenheim High School

Dogs - Pantoum

There are many different dogs
Dogs like the parks
They like jumping over logs
And have loud barks.

Dogs like the parks
They are big and small
And have loud barks
And are short and tall.

They are big and small
And are very cool
And are short and tall
They chase a ball.

And are very cool
They like jumping over logs
They chase a ball
There are many different dogs.

Joseph Wiltshire (12)
Blenheim High School

I'd Rather . . .

I'd rather be a boy than a girl.
I'd rather be a jewel than a pearl.
I'd rather be small than tall.
I'd rather be cooler than cool.
I'd rather be a rabbit than a pig.
I'd rather be little than big.
I'd rather stay home from school.
I'd rather be real than a wall.
I'd rather be a zombie than a witch.
I'd rather be poor than rich.
I'd rather be fast than slow.
I'd rather be a toy than Play Doh.

Jack Bates (11)
Blenheim High School

My Family - Pantoum

My family mean the world to me
My mum has two sisters and a brother
But my dad has a huge family
But I know all their names, one way or another.

My mum has two sisters and a brother
All those cousins, uncles and aunts
But I know all their names, one way or another
And I remember names by using poems or chants.

All those cousins, uncles and aunts
At family parties we all squash up
And I remember names by using poems and chants
It feels like we're packed into a cup.

At family parties we all squash up
But my dad has a huge family
It feels like we're packed into a cup
My family means the world to me.

Hannah Everett (11)
Blenheim High School

My Nan

She has a voice like a mouse,
She is as short as a pen,
She has flat ears like a pancake,
She has wobbly knees like tomatoes.

Olivia Doble (11)
Blenheim High School

Winter - Pantoum

Winter is cold
Wrap up nice and warm
Most of the leaves are really old
White snow is laying on the lawn.

Wrap up nice and warm
Snow as white as a wedding dress
White snow is laying on the lawn
Lots of Christmas prezzies, my house is such a mess.

Snow as white as a wedding dress
Nothing left on the trees
Lots of Christmas prezzies, my house is such a mess
Freezing my knees.

Nothing left on the trees
Most of the leaves are really old
Freezing my knees
Winter is cold.

Hannah O'Connor (11)
Blenheim High School

My Mate

My mate has a head as flat as a plate
My mate has a nose as long as a hose
My mate has legs as skinny as pegs
My mate has feet as flat as a seat
My mate has eyes as small as flies.
That's my mate.

Jake Cox (11)
Blenheim High School

Murder, Crime And Bad Behaviour

Murder, crime and bad behaviour,
May we bless the dead.
Every day someone's life is over,
Let it be on the killer's head.

May we bless the dead,
One bullet can end a life.
Let it be on the killer's head,
Many think they are forced to carry a knife.

One bullet can end a life,
Many people carry a gun.
Many think they are forced to carry a knife,
Playing with weapons isn't fun.

Many people carry a gun,
Every day someone's life is over.
Playing with weapons isn't fun,
Murder, crime and bad behaviour.

Joseph Larter (12)
Blenheim High School

Thunderstorm In The Cinema

It wished and whooshed through the doors,
Bumped and jumped the cinema seats.
It was a giant grey cloud sucking up the screen.
It went *crash, bang, boom!*
It was like a giant eating machine.

Lois Wood (11)
Blenheim High School

Summer - Pantoum

When it is summer and it's sunny
It is fun to play with water
In the water I am funny
Then there is no more water.

It is fun to play with water
While it lasts
Then there is no more water
But at least we had a blast.

While it lasts
We played in the sun
But at least we had a blast
Then we got out and went for a run.

We played in the sun
In the water I am funny
Then we got out and went for a run
When it is summer and it's sunny.

Callum Macarty (11)
Blenheim High School

My Little Sister

My sister has two blue eyes, like two bottle lids,
Her legs are as skinny as two thin sticks,
She walks and talks as loud as can be,
She is sweet, sweet as chocolate,
My sister is aged nine and I love her lots and lots.

Cerys Bristo (11)
Blenheim High School

Untitled

Football is energetic and fun
The best thing is to score
Most of the time I have to run
I would hate it if football was against the law.

The best thing is to score
It is great to see the ball in the net
It is harder when it pours
A goal is hard to get.

It is great to see the ball in the net
It fills me with pride
A goal is hard to get
When I score I like to glide.

It fills me with pride
Most of the time I have to run
When I score I like to glide
Football is energetic and fun.

Jordan Aldridge (11)
Blenheim High School

I'd Rather . . .

I'd rather be a girl than a boy
I'd rather be real than a toy.

I'd rather be a horse than a donkey
I'd rather be straight than wonky.

I'd rather have chips than beans
I'd rather be kind than mean.

I'd rather have queens than kings
I'd rather have arms than wings.

I'd rather have chocolate than a carrot
I'd rather be me than a parrot.

I'd rather be a mansion than a shed
I'd rather be alive than dead.

Rosie Weston (11)
Blenheim High School

Today

And as I wait for the first move,
My heart misses a beat.
And as a bullet screams in the air,
I can't feel my feet.

And as I aim and fire,
It hits the enemy in the head.
He falls and flops to the ground,
It's obvious he's dead.

But that was yesterday . . .

And as I stand on the muddy ground,
The enemy do the same.
I shake hands with people,
I thought were insane.

And as we smile and laugh,
Face to face,
I think will this stupid war,
Destroy all the human race?

But soon Christmas Day will finish,
Everything ends.
I never will see again,
My funny German friends.

Tomorrow more lives will be taken
And all will be the same.
I shall cry again at night,
It's all such a shame.

You may find in life things are bad,
But everything will be OK.
Yesterday, today and tomorrow,
Make the most of today.

Alice Green
Blenheim High School

The Hurricane

The hurricane blows so hard and strong
It tears around at one hundred miles an hour
But America is where it belongs
And it rips down any tower.

It tears around at one hundred miles an hour
It makes an extremely loud crash
And it rips down any tower
And it moves in a flash.

It makes an extremely loud crash
Its thunderous sound
And it moves in a flash
And the hurricane is city bound.

Its thunderous sound
But America is where it belongs
And the hurricane is city bound
The hurricane blows so hard and strong.

Jack Bacon (11)
Blenheim High School

December

The snow is droplets of cotton wool falling from the sky,
The brown crispy leaves are melting brown sugar on an apple crumble,
Frozen ice on the long winding roads,
Winter breeze of a cold freezer,
The woolly hats and gloves are a warm radiator.

Laura Wood (11)
Blenheim High School

Peace

War rages worldwide
Within hearts and minds
Maiming our souls

Guns, weapons and bombs
Instil torture and fear
Taunted, hated and confined
No wonder we retaliate

Claiming land we cannot see
Discriminating strangers who enter our land
Fighting for an injustice
When fighting itself is unforgivable

Brother killing brother
Can't we feel the peace?
Radiating from God in all forms of life
Contaminated by anger and greed

Look up
See the stars
Smell the flowers
Taste the honey
And feel the peace sent from above

Start within you
Heal your infirmities
Cleanse your soul
Close your eyes
And pray for peace.

Barbara Reddiar (14)
Coloma Convent Girls' School

Sounds And Sights Of The Island

The sound of waves,
A cold, dark cave,
A snow-topped mountain,
A water fountain,
A rumbling sound,
Oh when will we be found?

A big lump of compost,
For the souls that were lost,
A village for us to sleep,
While others secretly weep,
The blue sea surrounds us,
This whole thing strengthens our trust.

A fire is burning,
My head is turning,
A forest is here,
I'm starting to fear,
That we will not be found . . .

Sam Hill (13)
Coulsdon High School

Castaways

We're castaways washed up on this land.
The cool blue water splashing on the golden sand.
The monkeys swinging from tree to tree.
The shipwreck's sinking into the deep blue sea.

The sun just basking on the ground.
It's so hot you don't make a sound.
The blue finch singing a sweet song.
I hope I won't be here for very long.

The dolphin diving into the blue.
No one on this island but me and you.

Tanuja Singh (13)
Coulsdon High School

I'm So Lonely

It's so peaceful, far too quiet,
I'm all alone, by myself.

Hours ago I was with my friends
Laughing and joking to no end,
Look at me now, trapped by the sun,
Wishing that I had someone.
I'm scared to move from my spot,
Just in case I find a lot.
A lot of animals, that move in the dark,
Dogs that do more than bark.

It's so peaceful, far too quiet,
I'm all alone, by myself.

I turn around to see if it's only me,
But all I see is palm trees and the salty sea.
My heart's beating far too fast
I'm nowhere near home,
I've never been anywhere on my own.
I wonder what would happen if I close my eyes to breathe?
Would I ever see my daddy, would I ever leave?

Shanice Ryan (13)
Coulsdon High School

Help!

I'm trapped on an island, what shall I do?
There's no one here, except for me and for you.
I can hear the parrots squawking in the trees,
I can hear the squawking form furry monkeys.
I'm scared, *Help! Help! I'm begging you please.*
I'm collecting food and bits of bamboo,
So I can start a fire, and a snack for two.
I can smell the fruit, and the sea's seasalt,
I can smell the smoke, so I come to a halt!
I'm scared, *Help! Help! I'm begging you please!*
No reply . . . ?

Rochelle Faust (13)
Coulsdon High School

Lost Forever

Lost forever . . .
What shall I do?
I don't know where I am
Everything's new.
Brand new surroundings
Trapped by the sea
Golden sandy shores,
This isn't for me!
Sun beaming down
On my sensitive skin
My happiness faded
The sadness rushes in.
Filling my body up,
With unhappy times.
Tears grow in my eyes,
Anger spins round my mind.
There's a hole in my head
My stomach's stuffed with fear,
I want to go home!
I don't want to stay here.
I want to watch the TV
And sleep in my bed.
Eat my mum's dinner . . .
But I'm stuck here instead!

Isla Perry (13)
Coulsdon High School

Island

I've crashed on the sand,
Of a faraway island.
The plane's gone down,
I feel like a clown.
Can someone give me a hand?

James Regan (13)
Coulsdon High School

A Poem About The Island

The island is so beautiful
extravagant and exotic
but behind this fantastic land
is something so chaotic.

You never know what is sand
or what is quick sand
you never know where the caves
will lead you.

You never know what is lurking
in that rainforest.
You never know who or what
is living in that abandoned town.

The island is so beautiful
extravagant and exotic
but behind this fantastic land
is something so chaotic.

Lauren Bailey (13)
Coulsdon High School

One Way Ticket To Death

The screams and the horror,
The blood over my collar.
Cuts all over my face,
What is this place?

The cry of a child,
His death sealed and filed.
He takes his last breath,
He finally meets his death.

The intense heat keeps hitting my face,
My heart starts to race.
Smoke climbing the sky,
I wonder if I'm going to die.

Jack Ball (13)
Coulsdon High School

I Want To Go Home!

Where am I? What is this place?
It's as scary to me as outer space.
I feel deserted, I'm all alone,
There's only me and an age-old stone.

I drag myself up and look around,
There's nothing here, not a sound.
I sit against a palm tree and start to cry,
Why am I here? I might as well die.

I'm here by myself,
I wish I could just pick up the phone,
And hear their voices once again,
Or write them a letter with a dodgy old pen.

The things I want are not going to happen,
We'll never eat ice cream or take the tube to Clapham.
So I curl into a ball and await death to take me,
What did I do to make God hate me?

Charmaine Prentice (13)
Coulsdon High School

My Island And Me

My island is beautiful,
My island is small but full of life,
My island is perfectly formed like golden dew in the deep blue water,
My island sings a sweet song of love and grace as she lashes shores,
My island is always in my heart, it is my heart, it is my soul,
My island is a part of me, me and my island.

Ciara Williams
Coulsdon High School

The Island

On the island I stand alone,
Watching the lovely view,
As the navy blue sky turns pink,
While I think of you.

I am lost on this island,
Not quite sure where,
Being deserted,
It is just not fair.

I look at the sea,
It seems so clear,
I wonder if anyone knows,
The plane crashed here.

As the sun sets above the sea,
Why did this have to happen to me?

Louise Francis (13)
Coulsdon High School

The Island: Alone

My heart is thumping,
My blood is pumping,
It's trickling down my face.
My throat is dry,
A single tear in my eye,
I'm lost without a trace.
The smell of Hell,
The judgement day bell,
It's ringing louder in my head.
My short life has ended,
What's broken cannot be mended.
For my sins, God is unforgiving,
So take my life, there's no point in living.

Holly Burraway (13)
Coulsdon High School

The Island Poem!

The island is where all
Your dreams come true.
The island is where
Nothing bad happens to you.
As you stare in amazement
You wonder why you couldn't be there earlier.
As you look around all
You can see is the glistening blue sea
Crashing on the golden soft sand.
As the dolphins jump out the sea
You wish that you could jump in the sea
And swim like a dolphin.
The island is where all
Dreams come true.
The island is where nothing
Bad happens to you.

James Francis (13)
Coulsdon High School

Island Poem

Day by day the tension rises,
Starting to become hungry,
The group begins to split,
When will someone rescue us?

Exploring the island, confronting animals,
I begin to get scared,
I want my mum to come and save me,
I feel all alone.

Finding food proves difficult,
Trying to catch the odd wild boar,
Finally caught one and cooked it,
But the taste was extremely poor.

Mason Weston (13)
Coulsdon High School

The Island

I'm alive, but where?
Sand, sea and palm trees
I can see.
What to do I don't know
Is anyone else alive?
Do I go looking
Or do I stay?

What else is here?
Is anything here?
Is this a dream
Or is this reality?
Please tell me this isn't my fate.

I guess I'm on an island
And going nowhere fast.
So better go looking for food
And see if anyone else is alive out here.

Danielle Linnane (14)
Coulsdon High School

Seasons

Seasons come around each year,
Bringing joy to everyone.
They come so quickly and so near,
The next minute they've been and gone.
In nearly every season,
There is always a big tradition,
Christmas, Easter, there's always a season,
Which do you like best? What hard decisions.
They come around each month so fast,
And they're different in every way,
Pity they don't last for long,
Except for Christmas Day.
I love them all for different reasons,
So, which is your favourite season?

Jessica Bailey (14)
Dunottar School

The Sea And The Beach

Under the sea where the dolphins jump
And the sharks are swimming about without sound.
Where the fish all swim and jump and bump
And the seals are swimming around.
Out on the beach where the children play
And the women are looking at guys.
Where people spray suncream all day
And everyone gets pestered with flies.
I lie on my pink and purple towel
With the sun beaming down on my back
And near my head a dog starts to growl,
And then the rain starts and we all have to pack.
We run to the car as fast as we can,
Taking with us a load of sand.

Lottie Husband (14)
Dunottar School

Fantasy

The dragons flew,
The riders slew
All evil and its work.

The five are blown,
The pathway shown
For good and all its worth.

Death and destruction,
Light and redemption,
All this just in books.

Pick up a novel
In your palace or hovel
And start your adventure today!

Thomas Penfare (13)
Glyn Technology School

Life Of The Tramp Bob

There once was a tramp named Bob,
Lived in a tree did he,
He sat there bored
For he couldn't afford
A TV.

Bob liked food,
He ate a pie,
Then Josh came along
And he sang a song,
To tell Bob he would die.

Tanvir came along,
He said, 'Hello.'
He said, 'Hi.'
Then he said, 'Bye,
I have to go.'

Bob was all alone,
Don played the trombone,
Josh ate French fries,
Bob swatted flies
And he listened to the phone.

Ben Senneck (13)
Glyn Technology School

Tiger Shark

Tiger shark! Tiger shark with your razor-like teeth
Patrolling the murky darkness beneath,
Who would suspect that silhouetted fin?
As it glides through the depths, there is malice in your grin.

Your bloodthirsty eyes searching for prey,
There'll be blood in the water by the end of the day,
Your great hulking body, so strong, yet so slight,
Killing all fish that enter your sight.

James Penfare (13)
Glyn Technology School

The Lotter

There was a child of Mary Potter
Who always hoped to win the lotter.
The lotter is a game of chance
Where one wins the chance to dance.
Dancing is a terrible sin
When one falls upon a pin.
So when Mildred Potter won the lotter
Her nephew, rather mad,
Thought her luck was very bad.
When he in turn won the lotter
He danced all night with Mrs Potter.

Cameron Maxton (12)
Glyn Technology School

Love

When your heart sings,
Love, a peaceful dove,
Love, when you develop wings,
Soaring up above.

When the stars smile
And you fly with them for a little while,
When your heart begins to pace
And it floats with airy grace.

When someone will die for you
And doesn't care how you look,
To make you feel happy when you're feeling blue,
A prince as courageous as a lion but as wild as a boar.

When your heart sings,
Love, a peaceful dove,
Love, when you develop wings,
Soaring up above.

Cathryn Antoniadis (12)
Nonsuch High School

Drift Away . . .

Crashing and rumbling,
Roughing and tumbling,
It sweeps over you like a very loud duvet.
In one ear and out of the other,
Taking everything inside your head with it
On the outward journey.
No, it's not a thunderstorm.

Heartrending, heartstring-tearing,
Tear-welling, mind-stirring,
Its path doesn't take it straight out again
But downwards to your heart.
Makes you feel helpless, hopeless, awful -
What are you doing here?
No, it's not disappointment.

Calming, sleepy,
Slow and dreamy,
Its turquoise tints will smooth you down.
It travels to every part of your body and unlocks it,
Loosens it, relaxes it, switches it off.
You feel like going to sleep.
No, it's not a sleeping pill.

Joyful and sunny
And yellow and funny,
The moment it enters your head, it's like water.
It rejuvenates you and switches you on.
You want to hop, skip and jump
And laugh and laugh and laugh.
No, it isn't country air.

Angry, sad, calm, happy - it can make you feel anything.
See what music does for you.

Alice Ahearn (12)
Nonsuch High School

Untitled

My heart thumps,
The spotlight appears.
I open my mouth,
But all is silent.
My heart thumps,
People fidget.
I take a step forwards
But nothing more.
My heart thumps,
Louder,
Louder.
The steady pace
Fills my ears.
My heart thumps
Faster,
Faster.
The still steady pace
Fills my ears
And I faint.
Never to be heard,
Never to announce peace.
We will carry on
With killing and war.

Kirsty Harrod (11)
Nonsuch High School

Sleep Deprivation

It's been five whole days now
Without any sleep
I've tried turning lights out
I've tried counting sheep

But what is the reason
As I do not know
For this sleep deprivation
Why is this so?

Call for help, call a doctor
I need medical advice
On how I can sleep
As that would be nice

I've used lavender on my pillow
And lemon zest
To help me to be comforted
As sleep is the best

Sleep is the best!
Sleep is the best!
I've a desire for rest!
Sleep is the best!

So two days later, I'm lying in bed
Trying to get to sleep
When suddenly I'm drifting off
I think I'm going to . . . *beep!*

Jennifer Williams (12)
Nonsuch High School

A Little Girl

A little girl sits cold and hungry,
A little girl sits all lonely,
No one to comfort her,
No one to feed her,
She has searched the streets,
She has found nothing,
She feels hopeless and in complete despair,
So now she sits still as death.

The paper bag she owns is wrapped around her,
Not keeping her warm but reminding her,
Reminding her her family is dead.

She prays for them to return to her,
Her prayers aren't answered.
Hour after hour she sobs and weeps
Until finally, she falls into a deep, deep sleep.
This little girl lives in Africa,
This little girl is just seven years old,
This little girl now feels no hunger,
This little girl is now sleeping forever . . .

Lydia Murtezaoglu (12)
Nonsuch High School

The Earth Is . . .

The Earth is boiling,
Boiling in a fiery cavern.
The world is scorching
On fire beneath our feet.

The Earth is cracked,
Tectonic plates dividing states.
The world is split,
Masses cracking and moving.

The Earth is diverging,
Plates parting in the sea.
The world is leaking,
Lava spreading out of ocean's trench.

The Earth is grinding,
Earthquakes with violent shakes.
The world is colliding,
Plunging into the zone of subduction.

The Earth is hurtling,
Tearing through a vastness of space.
The world is balancing
Suspended in nothingness.

Amy Tiri (13)
Nonsuch High School

Don't You Feel It?

Don't you feel it, can't you, won't you?
Hasn't something stirred, somewhere and somehow?
A film of distress, can't you see it, hear it?
It's too much, how can you take it or bear it?
We see the pictures, the pain, the fear,
The faces of the lost or the ones who have lost.
The images of destruction, terrified and terrifying.
Then us in comfort, wasting money and hoarding money.
Just take a moment to think and to wonder,
What if it were your family, separated or dead?
Then would you feel it? Would you? Yes, you must.
So help them to get back on track, donate, volunteer.
Do something to aid the world, something, anything.
The suffering and the death, stop it, end it.
You can do it, help them, save them.
Now do you feel it?
Do you feel the love?
The need?
The hope?

Lindsay Harrod (12)
Nonsuch High School

Huddled Shapes

Nights with stars shining bright bring alive the shadows,
See the things in dark ignored,
But in the light displayed.

I know not of these spooky shapes
Huddled in their cloaks.
But when revealed
They stare with evil eyes ablaze.

Despite their evil faces
I've tried to see their minds.
But huddled shapes stay hidden
Even in the light.
They shrink back in the shadows
When tried to be displayed.

So let them be ignored
Whilst skulking in the dark.
Leave them be for time
And wait for shining stars.

Glynnis Morgan (14)
Nonsuch High School

Pleasure

Every morning we awake,
In the sun's sweet glowing light,
But do we care, have we noticed,
The wondrous mystery of the night?

We always have our worries with us
And so we are too blind to see,
The radiance of Mother Nature,
The splendour of the chestnut tree.

But trivialities concern us,
We cannot appreciate the pleasure:
Of seeing a child laughing happily,
Not while near us there is golden treasure.

The pace of life is ever quickening,
It is inevitable that we forget
To look at the sky in perfect blueness
And wonder what may happen yet.

Then pity us, poor fools,
Ignoring all and each delight,
Every beauty that's on offer
Is pushed away, out of our sight.

There is not time for contemplation
On what we do not need.
Disregarding each sign and revelation,
Living at fast forward speed.

We cannot understand true joy,
When all we want is to destroy.

We only have this realisation,
When our time has come to fall,
That is the curse of our generation,
The bitter irony of it all.

Serena Collins (14)
Nonsuch High School

What's It Like?

To know what it's like to fly,
Ask the man in the wheelchair
Who spends his life bound to the ground,
But dreams of spreading his wings.

To know what it's like to breathe,
Ask the woman who nearly drowned,
Who gasped her last breaths with desperate hands,
But escaped the water's icy perils.

To know what it's like to see,
Ask the little blind boy,
Who feels the sun yet cannot see its rays,
But still has lost treasures hidden in his mind.

To know what it's like to cry,
Ask the impaired, the desperate, the lonely,
Ask the heartbroken, the different, the unknowing,
Ask the person next to you.

Hollie Irvin (11)
Nonsuch High School

At A Football Match

The teams are ready,
The crowd goes wild
And the whistle goes.
Kick, run,
Dodge, tackle,
Dribble, chase,
Pass, slide,
Shot, jump,
Goal!

John Hockley (14)
Philip Southcote School

Football Match

The team are starting,
The crowd roars,
The whistle blows.

Kicks, shoots,
Go Blues go, go Reds go,
Blues dodge,
Foul, penalty,
Shoots, slam.
1-nil.

The crowds are roaring,
The teams kick off,
The ball's passed,
Red shoots,
Missed corner,
Passed goalkeeper grabs,
Goalie pass, Blue
Dodge, kicks,
Blues shoots.
2-nil.

Christopher Buist (14)
Philip Southcote School

Go Blues

Run, dodge,
Kick, slam,
Go Blue, go Red,
Shoot, corner,
Kick, shoot,
Goal,
The crowd roar.

Jai Patel (14)
Philip Southcote School

World Cup Winner

The teams are ready,
The whistle shrills,
It is kick-off, come on the Blues,
They shoot and score.
The crowd roars,
The Blues are one-nil up.
The Reds start,
The whistle shrills,
The Reds run and dribble past the goal keeper and score.
One all, it's the 90th minute, 2 minutes left,
The Reds have given a penalty
To the Blues who shoot, goal!
It's two-one to the Blues,
The whistle blows.

Adam Leslie & Lee Stenning (14)
Philip Southcote School

Firework Night

The sky is black,
Stand back looking up,
Light the fuse,
Ssss, vroom,
Whizz, crackle,
Pop, bang,
The sky is lit,
Boom!

Ronnie Hughes, Michael Cole & Luis Pinto (14)
Philip Southcote School

The Cricket

The teams are ready,
The crowds are waiting,
The first man is on.
Southcote first,
Crack, hit, *bang*,
Run, one, bowl,
Six, *smack*, bowl,
Out, *splat*.

Kieron Carey (14)
Philip Southcote School

Gloves

And all that was left were her gloves,
Her pink gloves,
Her mink gloves,
And like her gloves, he was empty now she'd gone.

And all that she had left was his love,
His endless love,
Eternal love,
And his love was the reason she was gone.

And every morning when he woke he saw her gloves,
Her best gloves,
Her dress gloves,
And like her gloves, a part of her was near.

And every morning when she woke she felt his love,
Why love?
Goodbye love,
And his love filled her with bitter fear.

And she was his love, and they were her gloves,
Leave love,
Let me breathe love,
She left her gloves and was never seen again.

Eleanor Luery (18)
Reigate Sixth Form College

Then And Now

With every day that passes,
I know you less and less,
What started off a masterpiece
Dissolved into a mess.

I see how far we've come now,
Matured through numbing pain,
So long since this began now,
We've both outplayed the game.

The summer months have flown us by,
Where do we go now?
Where the light might fade to next,
Just show me some way how.

It's simply not a lot to ask,
We know it's meant to be,
But plagued by thoughts of her last wish,
I fear too late - where is she?

Our worlds apart, now untorn,
It all falls into place,
Once shattered dreams, now reborn,
I want to run the race.

Iron out the differences,
A clean slate to start fresh,
Our tales interwoven,
A tangled, clear-cut mesh!

The summer months approaching fast,
Don't care what comes next,
Living for the moment is what
I'll remember best.

The end around the corner now
Or never? We shall see,
But with each kiss, I make my wish,
That you will never leave me.

Oliver Wright (16)
Reigate Sixth Form College

The Rosebud Convention

Mercury breezes pouring forth,
Sweeping across the dusty plain,
Wiping clean the historic memories,
Rosebuds connecting like chains.

Eerie silences rule them all,
The atmosphere remains unchanged,
Septic organisms spreading amongst
The dead and/or the deranged.

A seeming full Rosebud Convention,
Tangled and knotted in time,
Speaking only notes of lust,
Chilly feelings crush the grime.

Imagination over reality,
Like fearful passages of hate,
Choosing the right door to progress,
Requires studying the marks on its gate.

Thorn bushes grapple and twist to light,
Eager to push their way through,
Human-sized walls and concrete embraces,
To climb up and fight along too.

Their nightmare continues,
This sightmare must live,
Only to return my lack of
Forestry as it writhes.

Red Saunders (16)
Reigate Sixth Form College

Cigarettes

My dreams are like cigarettes
When they are plentiful I hand them out for all to enjoy
I watch them burn and smoulder away in the hands of others
As they black their lungs with the decay of my life
Anything to get them away from my own world.

My life is like a cigarette
It glows and pulsates with the life between my fingers
If you burn my life away with your addiction
Find that my cancer lives on the inside of you
And the spark is not easily relit

My heart is like a cigarette
It burns with all the warmth of fire
It reeks of death but offers release from your life
Slow suicide within its chambers
And a forfeit parallel to the hands of fate.

I'd offer you a cigarette
But all mine are broken.

Rebecca Handcock (16)
Reigate Sixth Form College

The Treasure War

Lost in battle, searching for treasure,
The map is with Smollett to Long John's displeasure.
Fatality is rising, dropping in a lost waterfall,
The anger and strength, the fear and downfall.

Lost in a forest, hiding from the war,
From Smollett's fairness, but Long John wants more.
Stuck within an island, no way to go home,
The blood and the tears, the cries and moans.

The victim's eyes, the life is drained
The paleness and stillness, the victim's maimed.
As life twirls and drains like a plughole,
The darkness and shivers, the silence of the soul.

Sean Barry (11)
Wallington County Grammar School

Lost

She left.
She felt angry,
Feeling so much anger as if a waterfall was in her mind.
Clenching her hands into fist,
Tighter and tighter.

Not knowing where to go,
She kept on walking, walking.
Feeling as if water was flowing,
Running away from a thing she was scared of,
But yet she didn't turn to go back.

Anger walking her on,
Yet getting a little bit scared,
She kept walking,
Every step she took,
Getting more frightened, frightened.

Kept looking over her shoulder.
Every breath she took,
More hope left her body.
Trying to stay really calm,
She kept thinking, thinking.

Thinking of a plan,
A plan to get back, back.
Searching for people to ask for directions,
Feeling as though she was the only person,
The only person in the world.

Wanting to go home,
Yet she didn't know which way.
Then she saw it.
Getting up and running after it,
Faster and faster.

Fabio Carta (11)
Wallington County Grammar School

Vampire

Vampire,
A man of courage, great intelligence, strength and iron will,
The undead wampyr,
The vampire.

Vampire
Has lived on for centuries, form mortal man to Nosferatu,
Feeding upon the blood of the living,
The undead wampyr,
The vampire.

Vampire,
Strong and terrible
And he reigns alone, supreme,
The undead wampyr,
The vampire.

Vampire,
Merciless and cruel,
A pact was made, perhaps
His soul for the immortality of life,
The undead wampyr,
The vampire.

Vampire,
This is the enemy that has come amongst us,
This is the corruption that dwells in our midst,
The darkness that has taken root in our hearts,
The darkness that must be destroyed,
For if not it will surely grow and spread until it has consumed us all,
This is the undead wampyr,
This is . . . the vampire.

Tom Harrison (12)
Wallington County Grammar School

Going To War!

With long patience I have waited for this day,
This war will be such a war, that all others will seem like play.
They may have 20,000 good and strong,
But my men know they have to win, they can't go wrong.

With swords, daggers and bare hand we will fight,
Be it all day or be it all night.
With no choice of return, recede or flight,
All my men know there are only two choices in sight.
Win the war and be known as famous knights,
Or lose and be known as fools who fell from such heights.

Blood shall be spilt, a flood,
Pain; is all part of the game.
Victory is near; I can feel it in my beard.
'Tis important to remember the struggle is of the body as well as
                                                    the mind,
Crush their morale, then victory one is sure to find.

Sohail Khan (11)
Wallington County Grammar School

Lost

There stood ahead of me nothing,
Utter and complete darkness,
Merged together with the fatal silence that lay upon me,
How I was nowhere
From somewhere . . .

I was in a different world,
Full of dreaded sins.
It felt as if time was slowly ticking,
I had neither food nor water,
Yet I was afraid to suffer in silence.
For I was nowhere to be heard,
I was as weak as water;
I was *lost . . . !*

Daniel Rodrigues (11)
Wallington County Grammar School

Lost

I am lost,
In the Whitgift Centre.

There are annoyed shoppers,
Trying to run away from the persistent salesmen dotted
Around the shopping centre.

Other shoppers talking,
And going on with their daily routine.

Oh look, there is my friend Bert,
No just a lookalike with hair showing through his wooden hat.

I am as scared as a mouse,
Surrounded by thousands of cats.

I am like the small moon,
With the Earth and sun on either side of me.

Look there is my mum,
The next stop is to run like in a 100 metre race.

My stomach has stopped hurting,
Because I am getting closer to my mum.

We opened our arms
And shared our love.

Jaykishan Gudka (11)
Wallington County Grammar School

Lost

Fear flowed through my veins like a gushing river,
Flickering images of my childhood came back to me,
Filled with childhood dreams of possessing treasure,
Hatred burning up inside my heart.
Trees looming over me, shaking their branches menacingly,
Walking first, then running, stumbling, grazing my knees,
Gasping for air like a drowning man.
Muscles aching in my legs, but I ignored them, pushing on,
Sweat beads trickling down my face like tears of desperation.

Sam Nazarko (11)
Wallington County Grammar School

Lost

It is a constant battle,
Yourself on one side
And yourself on the other.

You are lost,
You don't know where to go,
Left or right,
Right or left.

Everything is a blur,
Anger, happiness,
Chaos, sadness,
Emotions running wild,
You are running like a child.

You are lost in thought,
Mind firing like a gun,
The water calming,
You have crossed the River Gerico
And you know
There is no turning back.

Asher Carr (11)
Wallington County Grammar School

Dracula

A mixture of fear and anticipation,
The night comes,
Darkness,
Shadows come,
The mist appears,
It comes
And with it Hell's monsters,
Blood has been spilled,
It feeds
And with it Hell's monsters!

Scott Fanner (12)
Wallington County Grammar School

Aeroplane Terror

A s we pass through the check-in, our baggage is checked,
E verybody wonders what this will affect,
R eturning from its destination our plane arrives,
O ff goes our plane, very smooth to our surprise,
P reparing for take-off the plane begins to shake,
L eaving for the runway and fear begins to make,
A n engine is starting, a fierce and mighty roar,
N othing can be heard but the power of engine four,
E verybody holds on tight as up the speed goes,

T ension lashes through the cabin as the plane gently flows,
E verything is squashed under the uncomfortable pressure,
R ising people get a drink and feel much fresher,
R ising through the sky, people are now up high,
O n comes the captain's voice and people let out a sigh,
R elief spreads through the cabin as the plane begins to fly.

Thomas Tawse (12)
Wallington County Grammar School

Lost

There he lay lost,
As silent as the motionless trees,
Wishing to find another life form
Away from the villainous crew.

Dreaming of being with his departed father
In the heavens Jim stood,
Feeling his horrors flooding away for good,
Smiling like a diamond in the golden sun.

Then with a crash
Jim awoke
To find gun bullets flying above.
How Jim wished to be out of this place,
Home with his beloved ones.

Alex Simpson (11)
Wallington County Grammar School

Lost

I'm lost on Treasure Island,
As I think of where I might be.
I'm lost within an acre,
An acre of hollow trees.
No matter where I'm going,
I fall upon my knees.

I'm running out of food
And I dream of distant places,
Because buccaneers surround me,
Wherever they may be.
As I rush through bushes,
Eyes are watching me.

Over, under, left and right,
I can hear my teammates scream and fight.
But put those tragic thoughts aside,
For my dreams will draw back darkness.
Dreams of family, love and care,
With thoughts of loneliness and despair.

Julian Chan-Diaz (11)
Wallington County Grammar School

Prometheus

All I did was give them fire,
Now I am tortured as a liar,
Chains restrain me as an eagle pecks my liver,
While humans bow and quiver,
My power of immortality saves me for tomorrow,
As my siblings weep in sorrow,
But Zeus' mind will not hear,
Power changed him,
For he is too arrogant to see,
That he must set humans free!

Sam Christy (12)
Wallington County Grammar School

The Futuristic Battle

A future battle, over war,
Tony Blair and many more.
But every battle has death and sadness,
This always leads to hatred and madness,
Super powered Pikey fighters,
Killing people with cigarette lighters.
Laser guns and laser tanks,
Needs a higher than high soldier rank.
Small Canadian mutant babies,
Specially built to kill lots of ladies.
With sharp toenails and atomic spew,
A thousand would never survive a few.
Adrenaline spurs the soldiers on,
When they met the aliens they're gone.
With scary large atomic bombs,
The sound is louder than a zillion gongs.
Yellow, red, orange and more,
Destroys soldiers with bloody gore.

George McTaggart (11)
Wallington County Grammar School

My World

On the streets a boy is killed,
In the alleyway a boy is robbed
On a bus a boy is bullied.

No one can stop crime,
Not even the ones we trust.
The world has changed
The world isn't the same
Many fear God, others don't.

One day they'll be caught,
One day they'll be in jail.
Another day they they'll learn
To be the good citizen they weren't.

Allen Ola (12)
Wallington County Grammar School

Lost In The Dark!

I came here last night in the rain
No food with me.
I go searching for food,
I find animals instead.

Guarding the food from me like an Alsatian with its bone,
I run away frantically in fear of them,
I'm lost now, I can't find my way back,
I hear an echo of me crying.

I say hello repeatedly,
I hear nothing in return.
I see a shadow of a wild beast,
I hear a rustle in the dark bushes of the night.

I'm scared,
I can't move.
I'm weak,
I can't move.

I see the shadow again,
I hear the sound again.
I see,
I hear.

It's a person.

Nimesh Patel (11)
Wallington County Grammar School

The Merchant

His few long, white, wispy hairs
and small beady eyes
hardly conceive his immeasurable power.

Those beady eyes were once
the eyes of an imperious
but still loving force.
They have shrunk though
with the demise of his creation.
All the love has been drowned by
hate and anger and alone
he rages like a bull.

Even though he has the power to change
he never would for that would be evil
to take away from others
for what man has done.

He even knows he'll have to create again
for eventually man will plunge
the world into darkness.

Despite his hate and anger and terrible knowledge
he still does what the merchant must do
to trade devotion with happiness
and evil with punishment.

Gogulan Karunanithy (13)
Wallington County Grammar School

Stranded

We wound up here last night,
With no supplies to keep us all right.

We were comfortable but scared at first,
Oh the climate was scorching hot,
The golden rays of the dazzling sun beating down our backs,
Producing beads of sweat dripping off us,
We had to drink water to quench our thirst.

There was a strange bellowing sound,
Coming from the swaying palm trees above the ground,
I wonder what was lurking around.

Our fears intensified, a tight knot in our stomachs like a raging volcano,
We were vulnerable in this isolated forest,
What would become of our fate?

We heard swift movement and rustling all around us,
At that sudden moment I became the leader,
Ordering everyone not to fuss.

I have to find my inner strength,
To get us all out from this terrible nightmare . . .

Dilan Patel (11)
Wallington County Grammar School

Dragon War . . .

The days of terror dawned upon us,
Happening too fast, too quick.
Bombs of pain descended stealthily.
It was a sad sight, men sacrificed by their own will for their country.
Wishing this was a nightmare I only found reality
Adrenaline surged through me.
I could not contain myself, I had to do it.
No way out.
'Kill the beasts, kill them all,' it was so simple,
Yet I didn't understand this new feeling I had,
It was revenge.
Not caring for myself but only for revenge.
Death and blood was past me.
I rose from the darkness
Into a world of pain and flame
Avenging my long-lost brothers.
I picked up my gun and ran into the blinding light,
Only to find death was waiting for me.
As I climbed my path through the sky, I looked down.
Nothing could stop this war.
Humanity was doomed against the dragons, at the edge of extinction
And hope was nowhere to be seen . . .

Sunmeet Kandhari (11)
Wallington County Grammar School

Hunted

They came last night
And gave us such a fright.
The bears of the island
Keeping all the food from us.

They came last night,
We watched them from afar
Until they came into sight
With roars that were like thunder.

Walking slow but coming fast
Through the trees that were hiding us.
The trees moved as though they were alive
With never a sound we crept away.

Through the trees we ran
And although we found the food
We did not want to touch it
And after that they came . . .

Amos Pang (11)
Wallington County Grammar School

The Day My Heart Broke

Lucy I'm disappointed,
Mighty disappointed.
The two of us I thought we got on tolerably well,
Well enough in fact,
But it seems I was mistaken.
You were honest and direct,
Thank you for that.
You may not have found a husband in me,
You've found a friend,
Who'll never let you down,
Whatever fix you are in.
I thank you,
Now I take my leave.

Edmund Ryan (12)
Wallington County Grammar School

My Death

I turned back to look out of the window,
The sun had almost set,
A line of darkness was rising up into the sky from the horizon,
Deepening, spreading, and in the dark,
A knot of blackness forming,
Hardening, tightening, my death
With ragged, tattered sails
Riding along the waves of darkness
A figure on the prow
Leaning towards me,
Hungry, eager,
Urging on the ship,
Then the waves rolled higher and higher,
They crashed about me,
All was drowned,
My death was here.

Danyal Naseer (12)
Wallington County Grammar School

Lost

I wander through the jungle of students,
High school has begun,
I must get to my next class,
I hope it will be fun.

I don't have a clue where to go,
My art class will be starting soon,
Where the class has gone,
I do not know.

I've found my way to the art department,
I've found my way too slow,
I've forgotten my smock by accident,
It's the fourth week in a row,
After school a detention is where to go.

Joseph Forrest (11)
Wallington County Grammar School

Vampire

As far away as can be,
In a foreign country,
There was a race,
With a noble face
And there was a man,
In this land,
Who was courageous and strong
And reminded people where they belonged,
Until he sold his soul,
To the one who has no soul,
The dark one,
The evil one,
From man to monster
And this he cannot alter.
There are many names,
That give this monster fame,
One of them is Nosferatu,
Wampyr,
Or, more commonly known,
Vampire.
They do not die,
But in their crypts they lie,
Until the night-time,
And let loose their horrible cry.
They are fed by the blood of the living,
Blood from human beings, and they become Nosferatu,
Wampyr,
Or, more commonly known,
Vampire.

Cameron Truscott (12)
Wallington County Grammar School

The Special Season

Everyone's favourite time of year,
Pulling crackers, drinking beer
Presents bulging in Santa's sack
That was one thing he didn't lack.

Baubles hanging, tinsel glistening
Stories told, attentive listening
Presents waiting, suspense in the air
A sly little shake, with great care.

Christmas Eve, so close yet so far,
Small kids waiting, for a toy car
Game Boys waiting under the tree
Hoping one of them is for me.

The night draws closer, ever so near
Santa's preparing his reindeer
The elves have been working away
To help fill up Santa's sleigh.

Children tucked up in bed
Christmas wishes filling their heads
As Santa draws near
Christmas is almost here.

In the morning turkey is smelt
Then all the presents are dealt
Hurriedly ripped open
Hardly a word being spoken.

Faces filled with glee
Now to dig in to the turkey
Christmas comes only once a year
But is always so full of cheer.

Josh Bell (12)
Wallington County Grammar School

Dracula's History

My ancestors have lived,
For many a year,
As the power of the land,
As fierce and proud nobles,
As protectors of life,
As true patriots.
From love of his country,
My father once said,
'I gave my blood to the rivers,
And earth of this land.'
It seems his blood has been wasted,
As the earth now crumbles,
With his castle and his glory.
Soon I will be the one to pass,
And give my blood to new green grass,
There will be no more in my line,
All dead and buried in our tombs,
I dream of living for evermore,
With my bride to be,
Whom I have not yet found,
But she shall soon be mine,
For all eternity.

Adam Asquith (12)
Wallington County Grammar School

Dracula's Side

I am alone,

A lone with solitude,
M y dream is that I find a companion,

A companion that I can share my eternity with,
L etting our hearts be filled with joy,
O ne that will truly see the real me and
N ight after night we see the numberless stars and
E very day horizons rolling endlessly beneath our feet.

Adil Butt (13)
Wallington County Grammar School

Dracula

The sun began to set,
We climbed high through the pass,
Mountains deep in red light,
Sky darkened,
The world in shadows,
The carriage stopped,
Cold,
Bitterly cold,
Ascended to Castle Dracula,
I saw a flickering light,
An unearthly light,
I left the path,
Climbing towards it,
But then,
It vanished,
Making my way back to the path,
In the woods,
I saw a figure before me . . .

Oscar Ford (12)
Wallington County Grammar School

Looking Out To Sea

As I sit here on this sandy beach
Looking out to sea as far as the eye can reach.

I can see fishing ships bobbing
Along with the coastside factories throbbing.

The boats are rocking from side to side
With the ebbing, flowing tide.

I sit in my vantage point looking out into the great, big, blue abyss
It is bliss.

With none of the Earth's many evils there
To take their vice-like hold.

Ben McLellan (12)
Wallington County Grammar School

The Storm

Yesterday
A sudden, violent storm,
Most ferocious this town had seen.

At the height of the storm
A ship was seen,
With all sails set,
Making the harbour,
Caught by the gale.

Despite wind and rain,
Many people gathered
All with anxious hearts.
The ship tossed this way and that,
Many times disappearing
Only to reappear to the cheers of the crowd.

But against all odds
The ship weathered the storm
And at last drew to harbour.
As it came closer there was no man,
No crew, or in fact no soul
Manning the ship,
Just a dead corpse
Who steered the boat in . . .

Joshua Castle (13)
Wallington County Grammar School

Lucy Under The Vampire

Living life between waking and dreaming,
Not knowing which was which.
Soul being drawn from my body,
Days, a thickening mist all around me.
Nights filled with fear with claws scratching the glass.
Once a sweetness filled the room destroying the fear,
But then it went and fear returned stronger than ever.

Nothing they do,
Nothing they can do,
Nothing but fear at night,
Nothing but mist in day.

See the sun set,
See the sky grow red and the earth go dark.
Out of darkness he comes,
A mist creeping along the earth.
Cold fingers, reaching for my heart,
Squeezing it,
Squeezing it tight.

At the window he stands,
Waiting for entrance.
The same,
Always the same.

Christopher Godwin (12)
Wallington County Grammar School

Renfield

My master has come,
I'm ready to do your bidding,
He's come with the storm,
He summoned it, it brought him closer to me,
He will reward me,
Life, eternal life,
Life is blood . . . and blood is life.

It mustn't escape,
There shall be many,
You hear them,
Buzzing,
Buzzing,
Life, the box is full of life,
Fat flies filled with life,
Spiders eat flies, birds eat spiders,
A spider,
A spider is what I need,
For birds,
For blood,
For life . . .

Tom Housden (12)
Wallington County Grammar School

War

How would you feel
if you lived in fear
of dying every day for years?

What would you do,
scared to walk out of
your own front door in case you get killed.

You have no way of knowing
if your family or friends
will have survived the night.

Confined in a small underground hole
with people stuffed in any space around you
not aware how long until you come out, if ever.

No cosy bed to sleep in,
but a cold, hard shelter floor
and sounds of bombs and overhead planes.

Hundreds dying every day,
could be you, your friends, your family,
helplessly lying on the street.

None of this to be blamed on us
but the person who declared war is at fault.
Why do we have to have wars?

Tom Wainford (13)
Wallington County Grammar School

Save The World

Every car that passes,
Every light that's on,
Each barbecue that's lit,
Each crisp packet you eat.

Pollution is killing the world,
The world is toxic,
Nobody cares
For the next generation.

People getting mugged,
Houses being robbed,
Graffiti on the walls.

Pollution is killing the world,
The world is toxic,
Nobody cares
For the next generation.

People walk in fear,
The ice caps melting,
Shops go broke,
Penguins lose their homes.

Save the world,
Do your bit,
Everyone could help
To save the world.

Nihar Majmudar (12)
Wallington County Grammar School

The Trenches

The guns are pounding,
Killing my friends,
But still we stand there,
Awaiting our turn.

The guns are pounding,
We're getting ready,
To charge the enemy
And meet our deaths.

The guns are pounding,
All around me now,
I'm running as fast as I can,
One stray bullet will end me.

The guns are pounding,
What am I doing?
I'm running through no-man's-land,
With no confidence.

The guns are pounding,
I reach the enemy,
Fire my gun in all directions,
I drop to the ground, dead.

The guns aren't pounding,
The noise has stopped,
I feel no pain
And now I'm with all my friends.

Tom Kindler (13)
Wallington County Grammar School

Clothes

I wake up in the morning,
With my pyjamas on.
It's Monday today, a new school week,
I put on my uniform and yawn.

I get to school, see all my friends,
Chat about the World Cup.
A teacher comes in, it's the Deputy Head,
'Do your top button up!'

Before lunch, I have PE,
Put on my shirt and shorts.
We warm up by running round the field,
Then play on the tennis courts.

It's the end of the day, I'm on the bus,
I take off my tie.
I get off before my friends,
Grab my bag, say, 'Bye.'

After school, I go to football,
Put on my kit and play.
Last time it got really muddy,
The stain's not washed away.

It's 8.30, time for bed,
Put my pyjamas on.
Read my book for half an hour,
Get under the quilt and yawn.

Michael Brockman (12)
Wallington County Grammar School

The Poem Of Pain

The pain in my arm,
Burning through my skin,
Trying to stay calm,
What have I done to deserve this punishment?

Beaten to a pulp,
Lying there in the rain,
Unable to get up,
All I can feel is pain . . . pain . . . *pain!*

My arm is bleeding to death,
My whole body feels numb,
The snow beneath my icy body,
Freezing me into an ice-cap.

Beaten to a pulp,
Lying there in the rain,
Unable to get up,
All I can feel is pain . . . pain . . . *pain!*

My back bruised,
My nose is bleeding,
So what shall I do?
Do I cry for help or die alone?

Beaten to a pulp,
Lying there in the rain,
Unable to get up,
All I can feel is pain . . . pain . . . *pain!*

Shatik Patel (12)
Wallington County Grammar School

Return Of Captain Long John Silver

No freedom to walk
No way of escape
I'm chained up here
Like a prisoner or ape.

The sky life's a misery
And isn't so different for me
Being tortured by pirates
Isn't so easy.

Tell stories, they say
Drink all the wine
Off with his head
It'll surely be mine.

The cold, restless sea
Looks up at my feet
They'll make me walk it
Oh before I jump my name's Pete.

I used to be on this ship
Long, long before
Being around a dead pirate
Isn't half cool!

Salman Shahid (12)
Wallington County Grammar School

The Clumsy Detective

He doesn't have balance
He doesn't have co-ordination
He doesn't have eyesight
He doesn't have self assurance
He does have clumsiness!

He always forgets umbrellas when it rains
He always forgets his magnifying glass when investigating
He always forgets his identification card when going into
                                    police territory
He always forgets a wig when going undercover
He always remembers his clumsiness

He never knows what he is investigating
He never knows what to deduce
He never knows where to look
He never knows what clues he's looking for
He only knows how to be clumsy

Some say he is stupid
Some say being a detective is not a good career for him
Some say if he didn't have tobacco he would be a wreck
Some say his relatives are ashamed of him
But everyone knows he's *clumsy!*

Ryan Dansie (12)
Wallington County Grammar School

Holidays

The airport is near
The holiday is almost starting
All the bags are checked in
A panic begins as the plane is about to leave
The plane rises and rises

As the plane lands people rush over to get you off
All the passports are checked
You can finally leave for your hotel
People are taken away to get to their rooms
The room is massive
The holiday is starting well

Buses appear to take guests to the town
Where do we eat?
Where is everyone else going?
What menu looks the best?
Which is the most welcoming?

An enjoyable meal is had
The town is fantastic
There are shops in every space that can be found
The bus arrives again
You can go back and have a sleep

The pool is fabulous
You can swim for the whole of the day
The lunch is sent to the pool
The food is lovely

The holiday is nearing a close
A coach has to take you back to the airport
Check in takes place again
The plane takes to the sky
The holiday is unfortunately finished.

Luke Davis (12)
Wallington County Grammar School

Weather

Pounding you to the wall,
No point trying, you're bound to fall.
But now and again, there's a gentle breeze
Just cold enough, you're not going to freeze.
I bet you're wondering what it could be?
Open your eyes, and wind you'll see!

It covers everything in sight,
Making it all white and bright.
You can throw it around and have lots of fun,
But beware it's slippery so don't try to run.
I bet you're wondering what it could be?
Open your eyes, and snow you'll see.

Whether it falls down fast, whether it falls down slow,
Make sure you take an umbrella wherever you go.
And if you forget, you can surely bet,
You're going to get really wet.
I bet you're wondering what it could be?
Opening your eyes, and rain you'll see!

Bright as a star, quick as a flash,
Seconds after you'll hear a crash.
It makes the sky appear really nice,
You have to look quick, it doesn't strike twice.
I bet you're wondering what it could be?
Open your eyes, and lightning you'll see!

It is very bright, and provides us light,
It gives you a reason to have a water fight.
When it comes out, there is no doubt
You will eat ice creams to help beat the heat.
I bet you're wondering what it could be?
Open your eyes, and the *sun* you'll see.

Vinesh Solanki (11)
Wallington County Grammar School

The Day I Scored The Winning Goal!

The day I scored the winning goal
Is the exciting poem about to be told
It will always stay in my soul
The day I scored the winning goal

On the night before I started yawning
So I went to bed and started snoring
I dreamt about glory and fame
Little did I know it would happen in the game

On a cold and damp September morning
We travelled down to London with the rain still pouring
I was nervous but ready
But had a splitting headache

The game started and the opposition were strong
But somehow we managed to hold on
In the last nervy minute the wet muddy ball fell to me
I swooped past tired defenders and saw what could be

I sprinted through the gap
And then suddenly heard a snap
I played on and flicked it past the keeper into the goal
And that's when I was the hero
Because I scored the winning goal!

Samuel Chislett (12)
Wallington County Grammar School

The Slopes

Down the mountainside like a silver bullet;
Whoosh!
With two slender skis and a pair of sticks.
Slaloming with the pace and control of a falcon.
Trailing snow through the air as you fly off a jump;
Whoosh!
Pain attacks as you lose control
And you brace yourself for the minute of cold blindness.
Whiteout on *the slopes!*

Straps on the feet at the top of the piste,
Click . . . click
You snap the board round and prepare to take off.
Steady as a mountain goat at first but as you gain speed,
You feel your straps loosen and approach a jump,
You bend down and attempt to fasten your strap,
But you're losing altitude quickly.
Cli-crash!
You roll, but your board is still attached.
You feel your legs
Snap!
With the tension.
The air-ambulance is called.
Injury on *the slopes!*

Sam Worrall (12)
Wallington County Grammar School

The Foggy Streets Of Time

Running through the streets of time, the fog is getting thick
Pushing through the haze to escape this terrible place
Buildings standing tall, windows flashing in the sun
The streets are paved with concrete
Nothing lives in this empty city
Then the buildings begin to change
Slight changes
A little moss growing here and there, weeds poking through the floor
One catches my foot
Falling
Hitting the ground, jumping up, running on
The fall of the stone empire, the concrete jungle
The reign of the plants begins
Buildings crumble, crashing into the ground
Trees shoot out of the ruins, the path wears thin
Trees attack the lone human
Branches shoot out to block the route
They are easy to avoid
Jumping over obstacles, breaking through the trees
The portal gleams ahead, but begins to shrink
Into the clearing, the fog has cleared
Full speed
Touching the portal
Being sucked in - legs, body, arms, then finally head
Safe at last!

Joseph Wilson (12)
Wallington County Grammar School

Space

At night, looking up into the never-ending sky.
Space.

All the tiny eyes shimmering down on me.
I begin to wonder,
Stars born so long ago,
Why did it take them all this time to see our wonderful world?
The moon floats nearby in mid-air,
Like a boat on the ocean.
I look around and there's always something new,
A star I haven't counted,
Or a strange misty colour, drifting lightly.
The Milky Way draws out a faint line of colour,
Across the blackness.
What are all these amazing things?

Staring even further,
I wonder what's up there.
Maybe there's another creature,
Looking down on me.
What is out there?
Does the universe just stop,
Or does it keep on going?

The day soon comes.
The blanket of darkness that covers the sky slowly unfolds.
The peacefulness of the night
Disappears into the light of the new day.

Tom Diamond (12)
Wallington County Grammar School

Desert

A haze of heat rises off the baking sand,
The temperature scorching,
Like a torrent of fire eating up the land.

Voluminous cloth flutters in the gentle breeze,
A masked man rides by,
A glimpse of a jewelled dagger by his side.

The great sand dunes,
Like waves of a frozen ocean,
Trying to conceal the horizon.

A gentle hiss and slither,
Of the scaly reptiles basking in the midday sun,
Ready to pounce on any creature passing their way.

Soft pad of camel hooves,
High-pitched cry of the desert eagle
And the gentle scurry of rats across the plain.

A distant oasis shimmering,
One last scrap of hope,
Only to be shattered as it fades away from your imagination.

Joe Williamson (12)
Wallington County Grammar School

Rugby Means War

We, the players, huddle in our changing room,
Ready for the game, gathering a team spirit,
Ready to play our hearts out.

The whistle blows, we kick for ten,
Our men they run, but the opposition beats them to it.
The scrum, drive hard, our bodies strain,
The line-out's brutal, the backs, dummies in vain.

Half-time blows, we are all relieved,
Soon time is up, we're back in the game.
The opposition vulnerable, it's time to strike,
The lock runs, at full pelt,
He catches the ball, stays low and drives.

The ruck clears, the ball is nowhere to be seen,
Suddenly it is found, halfway down the wing.

The back, he passes and the hooker catches,
He dives, scores the try,
The conversion won, 7-0
The whistle blows, we're victorious!

Joe Henderson (12)
Wallington County Grammar School

The Day My School Burnt Down

One day my school burnt down,
And the fire did surround.
Me and my mates were finally free
And now no school for me!

At first we wondered what to do
But then we headed to a life that was completely new,
And this was the key
There was no school for me!

First we headed to get a Big Mac
Now we had been cut some slack
I could clearly see
There was no school for me!

We came to the park
Played football in the dark.
I went to have tea
There was no school for me!

But now this is not as cool
And I wish that I could go back to school
But the problem that I see
Is that there is no school for me!

Edward Stedman (12)
Wallington County Grammar School

The Boy At The Back Of The Class

That boy at the back of the class,
Just stares all day long
As blank as a sheet of A4 paper.
Staring into the world,
Just staring . . .

That boy at the back of the class
Is not extremely bright,
But as soon as he's asked a question -
'Please Miss, $E=MC^2$!' He always gets it right.
Most of the time he seems half asleep, then pounces in for the kill . . .

That boy at the back of the class
Slouched there, in his chair,
Is scribbling a note, extremely fast, but looks very neat.
He then folds his note perfectly into a B9745 paper aeroplane
Then glides it into my hair
Quickly but carefully I unfold it . . .

'Oi, stop staring at me Stupid!'
Immediately my thoughts have flicked
From being a nobody to the . . .
Bully my friends have warned me about!
That boy at the back of the class,
An enemy I picked . . .

Dominic Simpson (11)
Wallington County Grammar School

Music

There are many types of music
Too many that we can't name
That is why I love music
It's the name of the game

From MCs to rock
From R&B to metal
And even from the music loved by Spock
It's all like an overheating kettle

From ballads to hip-hop
From country to trance
It gives me a bop
And makes me want to dance

Music is like a knife
It could be your life
Music is fun and zest
Music is the best.

Simon Preston (12)
Wallington County Grammar School

Stars

Stars, stars in the sky
Stars, stars, please don't die
Stars, stars shining bright
Stars, stars, some take flight.

Black holes dark as night
Black holes suck in light
Black holes like spaghetti
Are lost in an endless jetty.

The galaxies are wondrous things
It is there where the angel sings
Space is endless, just like school
And bullies are quite easy to fool.

Christopher Mann (12)
Wallington County Grammar School

The Lure Of The PlayStation

It lies in the corner innocuously,
The magical black box beckoning me,
Leave your homework,
Come play!

Plug in, switch on and whirr away.
What shall I tackle today?
Football, war games or adventure quest?
Think - what do I like best?

Adrenaline rushes, excitement abounds,
Graphics to die for and magical sounds,
Mouth dry, fingers flying, fighting a giant dragon,
I must, simply must get that last golden flagon!

Time slips away as I'm lost in this world
Of mythical creatures and knights of old.
At last my quest is completed, no more mazes to follow,
(*Oh no!*) English homework is due in tomorrow!

Matthew Bieda (12)
Wallington County Grammar School

Everyone Is Different

Some people are big,
Some people are small,
Some people are short,
Some people are tall.
Whether we are black or white,
There is one thing in which we can unite,
That underneath our outside shell,
We all can feel and touch and smell,
The world around us, however mad.
We all feel happy, we all feel sad.
But one thing of which we can be sure,
Everyone is different!

Harry Palmer (11)
Wallington County Grammar School

Fifteen

Andy Warhol said,
'In the future, everyone
Will be famous for fifteen minutes.'
Fifteen minutes of fame -
How shall I play the game
To see my name shine?

Join the fast-paced, rat race,
Hurly-burly, hurry, rush,
Treadmill, do-it-now,
Non-stop, power push.

Catch the camera, grab the action,
Win the match, kick the ball,
Write a book, star in a film,
Work, work, work! Have it all -
For fifteen minutes.

Or shall I spend,
Fifteen minutes quietly -
Looking into the future
And saying 'Let it be'
As the nation sang in the new millennium;
And let time pass
In the way meant for me.

Shall I play the game
For fifteen minutes of fame
Or wait patiently
For my time to come?

Calum George (12)
Wallington County Grammar School

The World Today

The world today is a dreadful place
Some people have to live on the street
Without food and no place to say grace
For there is evil but there is no sweet
Because there is not enough for me to eat
The world can be a dreadful place

The world today is a brilliant place
With lots of money to bet on a race
Everyone has a house with a door
Because hardly anyone I know is poor
For the world is a brilliant place

The world today is a complete mess
I'm so tired it's giving me stress
My family cannot take it anymore
Because of army troops coming ashore
I think we may be no more
For the world is a complete mess

The world today is a normal place
Sometimes people live unfairly
We have to be quite wary
Some of us have a glorious life
With a lovely wife
For the world today is a normal place

This is what some people think
About the world today
But certain people don't get their say
For the rich get the lot and poor get nothing
I believe that everyone should have something
This is what I think.

Ben Allan (11)
Wallington County Grammar School

The Christmas Season

The Christmas season is a joy to all.
An event distinguished throughout the world,
                              celebrated by every individual.
Our eyes widen with impatience and our souls scream with eagerness.
Oh Christmas is a sensational time!

Snow paints the dew-laden lawn and icicles droop from rooftops.
The bitter wind thaws our faces as we bustle here and there.
Moist air rises from our lips like a menacing dragon stalking its prey.
Squirrels dart from tree to tree, only to expose a final conker.

Shop prices reduce by a half and anxious children pounce towards
                              their expensive targets.
The succulent aroma of roasting chestnuts crams the humid air.
Christmas trees are all around, buyers competing for the largest.
Vibrant shades of every colour fill house windows to a
                              ridiculous degree.

The luscious odour of Mum's Christmas dinner: roast turkey,
Crispy potatoes and tender vegetables which skate
                              around your mouth.
The pleasant warmth of a roaring furnace, blazing to an excessive
                              desire.
The exciting crunch of St Nick's boots and the thrilling flare of his
                              scarlet coat.
His fluffy white beard tickles your face as he leans over your bed.

Your senses are enhanced as you hear the milk and mince pie tumble
                              down his throat.
Once you wake your heart starts to beat, you inspect your room.
You observe the wrapping paper and rip with all your might.
Yes! You've received the gift of your heart's aspiration.

Daniel Heffernan (12)
Wallington County Grammar School

My Shadow

I have a little shadow that comes in and out of me,
The point of this shadow is more than I can see.
The size of this shadow's from my foot up to my head,
It even jumps before me when I jump into my bed.

My shadow is my best friend and is always sort of cool,
But when he dances in front of my friends he acts like a fool.
My shadow is incredible and always makes me laugh,
He turns into tigers, elephants and even a giraffe.

My shadow follows me everywhere and is very hard to lose,
The only time I lose him is when it's time to snooze.
My shadow's very good at sports and has a good running time,
But every time I race him he's always an inch over the line.

My shadow's very naughty, and always does something wrong,
When the teacher comes and peers over me he's mysteriously gone.
My shadow likes to gossip and talks behind my back,
But when I anxiously turn around he's still behind my back.

When I see my shadow he's always on the ground,
The only time he jumps and dances is when I run around.
My shadow makes funny noises and always shouts aloud,
Everyone in my class turns to look at me as if I was the clown.

My shadow is a joker and that's just how he is,
When he goes and plays a joke it's always on my sis.
My teachers always look at me in some peculiar way,
Almost if they are suggesting that I be in detention in May.

My shadow likes to eat a lot and doesn't make a sound,
But when he's finished he burps out loud.
My mother then comes over and sends me to my room,
Even though it's not my fault I fear it is my doom.

I think that over all this shadow is my friend,
But when it's time to go to sleep and wake up it starts all over again.

Ciaran Alli (12)
Wallington County Grammar School

A Distant Memory

Inside the cobra's fang is the frequent, melodious sound of rainfall
Inside the rainfall is the maroon tang of its blood
Inside the cobra's blood are the many echoes of its long-gone victims
Inside the victim's cry are the smooth, dry snake scales
Inside the cobra's scales are slopes of sandy grassland
Inside the slope of grassland is the cobra's patterned hood
Inside the cobra's hood is the leafy foliage of the forest
Inside the leafy forest floor is a cobra's eye scattered with a
                                                                    bloodthirsty craving.
Inside the cobra's eye is a sandy bank
Inside the sandy bank is a cracked cobra skeleton buried by darkness
Inside the cobra skeleton are scratches and ferocious claw marks
Inside the claw marks are an ancient snake's fractured memories
Inside the cobra's fractured memories are a great battle
Inside the great battle is a puddle of cobra's blood, rippling in
                                                                    the breeze
Inside the puddle of blood is a reflection of a bloodied carcass
Inside the bloodied carcass is a cobra's curving, barbed fang.

Joe Heritage (12)
Wallington County Grammar School

Tree Trunk

T he tree that lay far away
R ose up to be a special species
E xcellent it looked with apples growing
E xpands on the grass that needs mowing

T he tree would lighten the children's faces
R oots spread from all places
U nder the soil which needed composting
N ear the tree you could feel the rough bark if you cut the tree
K illing the tree is not nice leaving the world empty and darkened.

Manoj Radhakrishnan (11)
Wallington County Grammar School

Rainbow

Colour, colour always different never two the same.
Red, blue, green and yellow.
Far too many colours to count.
Some may blend others may not.

Pink, green, purple and blue these are just a few.
Can be bold can be frail.
Red for anger not for peace.
Orange is the active one, definitely not the one to sit inside on
a sunny day.
Yellow, happy and bright a cheery sight, never sulking always at ease.
Green is the colour of life.
Blue is the colour of peace and calm, almost impossible to anger it,
can't catch it blowing its top.
Purple, the colour of the spirits, calm at times, easily angered.
Black never a good colour, death is its thing, once that comes about
you will hardly have time to say goodbye.
Grey is plain, grey is basic, very boring I have to say.
White is pure as the frosting snow.

Joshua Freeman-Birch (11)
Wallington County Grammar School

The White Stallion

In the countryside, there lies a beauty,
No one has ever seen.
Its white mane, silky soft, shines like silver.
Its mystic, yellow eyes see nothing but peace
And its unicorn-like horn as sharp as can be.
Its hooves are as hard as diamonds,
Its speed, the only word ins unbeatable.
It feeds on the flesh of plants
And its teeth like a razor, can cut through anything.
However, if none have seen this beast of beauty,
Where do these descriptions come from?

Hariharan Sri (12)
Wallington County Grammar School

Storm

The sky was calm at the beginning.

Then it darkened, clouds swarmed,
Their hulking grey bodies
Heavy with rain.
Thunder rolled,
Sounding across the sky.
Rain began to fall
Heavier and heavier,
Hailstones and sleet
Hammering down.
A flash of light
Darted across the sky
Illuminating all for a moment.

The bracken trees
The dark woods
Being beaten by raging winds.
Those winds they tore
Across the ground
Ripping up all in their path.

Another flash of lightning
Crackling through the air,
Strikes a tree
Ignites a tree
And burns a tree
Till it is no more.

The clouds shifted
Revealing blue.
The sun shone
Birds sang.

And all was calm.

Qasim Alli (12)
Wallington County Grammar School

The Horrible Sighting

Johnny rode down the road singing his song
Why it had taken him this long
Was it the people?
Was it the trees?
Or was it babies,
Crawling on their knees?

Johnny had seen such a dreadful sight
Worse than people in a fight
This was too much for his little eyes to bear
He could no longer seem to stare
Horror struck in his sight
And as for them
They laughed in delight.

Was he supposed to see what he had seen?
This was not right for a living being
Johnny was going through terrible thoughts
His little eyes looked distraught.
It was crushing his head
Was he in a dream?

Birds flew past
He looked at his feet
His heart was pumping ever so fast
Would he ever last?
He did not know
His conscience had got the better of him.

What he had seen
We will never know.
For this sight was terrible and never to be repeated
He pedalled as fast as he could go
Pumping with his little feet.

Sam O'Brien (11)
Wallington County Grammar School

The Wonderful World Of Books

I know a secret door into
A thousand scary places;
Where there's bloodsucking vampires
And things that don't have faces.

A time machine that takes me
To fight Sir Francis Drake,
And through breathtaking jungles
On a magic silver snake.

I can leap into the future
On the Starship Enterprise;
Or crawl into a rabbit hole -
Quickly changing my size.

I'm solving a murder mystery
You can follow if you dare:
While all that are around me
Think I'm sitting in my chair.

I'm flying just like Superman
Or riding painted wagons;
I'm eating food in palaces
Or killing fearsome dragons!

I met Alice and Verucca,
Gandalf and Captain Hook.
Oh, I do have an amazing time
When I sit and read a book.

Christopher Lynch (11)
Wallington County Grammar School

Bananas

Bananas are soft,
Bananas are nice,
I gobble them up,
But never think twice.

And as I sit at
Mum's kitchen table,
I suddenly become
Extremely unstable.

I run to the dustbin,
The sink or the loo.
I say to myself,
'I think I'm gonna spew.'

It happens so fast,
So very quick.
It's the kind of feeling
That makes you sick.

I will not speak
Of the dreadful end.
Because it's driving me
Round the bend.

So to this day,
I never eat,
Any bananas
Before tea!

Thomas Willis (11)
Wallington County Grammar School

Nature

Sometimes it shines on me in the mornings
Other times is throws water at me

Far worse can happen
Disasters that come now and again
But the people that suffer
They feel terrible pain

First there are earthquakes
They wreck everything from houses to beehives
But the people that suffer
Are the ones who lose their lives.

Then there are tsunamis
They drown people one by one
There's nothing left
Sometimes we wonder is God having fun?

Thirdly there are tornadoes
They tear everything down
They don't miss a spot
They've demolished the whole town.

Lastly come fires
They burn to ash
All the remains
They become trash.

Jay Ruparelia (11)
Wallington County Grammar School

Animals Of Britain

A is for ant small but strong
N ightingale, its voice strong and sweet
I is for inchas jo a small, beautiful butterfly
M is for mute swan, slow and graceful
A is for adder small but dangerous
L is for long-tailed tit, bright eyed and alert
S is for short-tailed vole, grumpy and loud.

Alexander Riley (11)
Wallington County Grammar School

The Animal City

It was a new day in the bustling forest
The bears were happily chatting
The birds were busy flying
The squirrels were frantically shopping
The moles were hobbling as usual

Teddy bear families were on their monthly picnic
Wild strawberry and chestnut sandwiches

Late for work, birds were in a mad rush
Annoyed at the late winds and breezes

Squirrel mums on their weekly shopping trips
Checking the nutritional value and brands of nuts

Elderly moles smelling their relaxing lettuces
Dreaming of yesterday's social hole club

In the human city people were hiding and snarling
Some hibernating in their homes
Others hunting for leftovers in bins
Most rushing back to their beds before nightfall.

Douglas Leeks (12)
Wallington County Grammar School

Bart Simpson

He's like a human prank book,
You name it, he's done it,
He's got lots of friends,
He's got a good family,
Homer strangles him,
Marge loves him,
Lisa hates him and
Maggie doesn't know.

Karan Patel (11)
Wallington County Grammar School

Chocolate, Chocolate And More Chocolate!

Mmm, which one to have, which one to have,
Ah there's my favourite, oh wait and there's another . . .

Choices, choices so many choices,
Wrappers so colourful, tempting and bright,
The creamy, dreamy chocolate,
Waiting to be devoured with all my might,
Milky white and melting brown and some as dark as night.

Choices, choices so many choices,
Slabs or buttons or chocolate shapes,
Some with caramel or fruit and nuts,
There's even chocolate in chocolate cakes.

Choices, choices so many choices,
I'm in Heaven, the taste so delicious,
I'm on top of the world!
So warm inside,
Pop another in my pocket to enjoy along the ride!

Samuel Pearce (11)
Wallington County Grammar School

The Truck

Sitting there, in the shaded truck
Knowing what I had to do
Waiting for my chance
Then I turned the key
The engine stirred
But still no movement
Then a shout from behind
'Put it in gear'
So I put the truck in gear
As the truck moved forwards, I was confident
But then as it struck a hole
I knew I'd mucked up!

Daniel McKeown (11)
Wallington County Grammar School

Autumn's Back

Trees dropping leaves again
Falling to the ground
Drenched by the rain today
Because autumn is back

Leaves rustle beneath my feet
The nights are much longer
Trees changing their colour
As we approach Christmas
Now the days get shorter
The temperature drops down

Autumn is coming back
Trees dropping leaves again
Falling to the ground
Drenched by the rain today
Because autumn's returned.

Michael Eglon (13)
Wallington County Grammar School

Birds

See the birds, flying so high,
How wonderful it would be to fly in the sky.
To dive down, upon your prey,
And eat and sleep throughout the day.
To be a bird, to be a bird . . .

To be the king of all the skies,
And be feared by all eyes.
To hunch up in a cosy nest,
And be envied by the rest.
To be a bird, to be a bird . . .

To be at the top of the food chain,
And carry on, even in the rain.
To be up there and ride the thermals,
And swoop around, in circles.
To be a bird, to be a bird.

Jacob Guest (11)
Wallington County Grammar School

Battle Of Strength And Magic

The frightful wind thundered,
The earth shook with mighty power,
A mage and a warrior locked in battle,
On top of the grand king's tower.

The mage grabbed his staff,
Chanted three powerful spells,
Harum-Anfa-Rasga,
And sent fire from the deepest hells.

The warrior drew his sword,
Drew his sword and shield,
This mighty cry came next,
'The magic sword I yield.'

The mage was very startled,
He knew the sword was great,
He summed up his current position,
Death would be his fate!

'Ha, ha, ha!' mocked the warrior,
He was certain he would win,
He drew up all his strength and might,
(But the mage didn't know that he was as weak as a pin).

The mage had one choice,
To unleash one final attack,
Summoned up all his energy,
And sent his spell, with a smack!

The warrior lay on the floor,
Defeated and dead,
The mage took the warrior's sword . . .
And brutally chopped off his head!

Daniel Lamb (11)
Wallington County Grammar School

The Power Of Love

The power of love is truly divine,
It spreads over the world like a sunshine.
The word love is affection
And if you don't have it you need protection.
The power of love can stop you from that sigh,
Because it will make your day and lift your head up high.
I really thank God for making love possible
Because a world without love would be truly horrible.
Do not go and take love for a joke
Because if you don't find it you're going to choke.
Love doesn't have to be a kiss,
You can show love to someone you just play with.
Love to a friend may sound sad,
But it lifts up their heart and makes them glad.
Even if you just say hello,
Truly inside it makes us glow.
If you love somebody like a heart with a bow
Really you should let them know.
Unfortunately there is not much love in the world,
If only they heard the message that I heard.
Jesus told us to love one another,
But instead we start killing each other.
Red is the colour of love,
But now it spells danger for us.
Now you know what I'm trying to say,
If you don't there will be a price to pay.
So just stop the bombing and all this war,
Because it was madness that people saw.
So just stop killing each other
Do what Jesus said to love one another.

Bradley Griffiths (11)
Wallington County Grammar School

Exams!

Exams, I hate them, everybody hates them but for kids it's worse,
we have them all the time!
They should scrap exams because I say, 'What good is it
doing for me?'
If they didn't have exams it would be good to see!
Then everyone would be happy and no one would complain,
Because for me the whole idea is just too lame!

Exams stress everyone out even the little kids of seven
But then comes searching schools, at the age of eleven!
I've been there, nearly everyone has, but deep inside
Everyone's heart, they know exams are too big of a stress.
So please someone scrap exams for everyone, because truly
they're not the best!

Someone take out exams, I know that's bad but for us kids
we'll be happy as a clown.
It's the only way to take stress away
*(So someone take those horrible exams out and
lock them up!).*

Akash Gajjar (12)
Wallington County Grammar School

Problems

Not enough food to go around
Hurricanes mean that people have drowned,
Guns and knives in every drawer
People die because of war,
Suicide bombers everywhere
But none of them could give a care,
Global warming causing trouble
The sea's so hot it's ready to bubble,
Whirlwinds whisking people away
These are the problems with the world today.

William Dunne (12)
Wallington County Grammar School

Nature

There are sweet smelling flowers bedded in the mud,
And crispy, crunchy leaves fallen from vast, huge trees,
Hidden inside the sleek petals is a colourful butterfly,
Under the crinkly leaves there crawls a tiny centipede,
Up high in the trees there's birds of all shapes and colours.

In the night there is no noise except for the hooting of a wise old owl,
And when the night becomes still the fox begins to forage,
The hedgehog snuffles around in search of slugs and other bugs,
Mice scamper in the dark, through the leaves and other foliage,
As the night turns to day the night-time animals hide away.

If we do not look after such beauty all will be of waste,
If we litter and do not take care of nature
It will be our downfall.
Protect, preserve and enjoy everything around us.

Sam Cooper (11)
Wallington County Grammar School

In The Future

In the future there will be robots
And giant monster trucks
About the size of a lamp post.
Children will go to war with evil teachers
And grandparents will wage war with aliens.
Presents will be free on every holiday
Including the day of finding,
For discovering the galaxy and beyond.
There will be people living on Mars, Jupiter and Mercury
17 new plants will be discovered by one eight-year-old.
People will also live under the Earth and above it!
Junk food will taste normal as usual
But it will be good for you
And last of all, I have no idea of the future
I've just made it up.

Nandu Sanilkumar (12)
Wallington County Grammar School

Lost

My mind has gone crazy,
I'm lost,
I don't know where I'm going,
I'm stuck in the middle of nowhere,
Nobody's here with me,
I'm all alone.

The trees are blowing,
They whisper to me,
'Go home before it's too late,'
As the day goes on,
I wonder whether I can get out.
Alive.

I stroll about everywhere,
Everything looks the same,
I feel as if I'm going round in circles,
Going to the same place over and over again.

I think there's someone watching me,
With their dark, gloomy eyes,
The bush wobbles and I fear that,
Someone will come out any moment now to pounce on me.

I start to run to get a head start,
A man comes out and sprints to chase me,
In my way though a tree trunk on the ground,
I jump and hope for the best.

I just made it, but he seems to float over the trunk,
He is catching me up I'm sweating now,
Wait I can see an opening,
I must be coming to the end.

I know where I am now,
Right in the park,
I can see my friends,
I look behind and the man disappears like a ghost.

Thomas Hornsey (11)
Wallington County Grammar School

Revenge

Hatred is swelling up inside me,
I have been betrayed,
If I don't release it I could create a holocaust
It's like solitary confinement.
I'm lost, lost in my words.

I'm lost in an enigma, a moral dilemma,
Revenge is what I want,
To avenge my father.
It is my destiny to do so.
I'm lost, lost in my thoughts.

I will find them cowering,
Detaining them will be pleasurable,
But I won't lose anything,
To kill will be a loss, to them.
I'm lost, lost in my emotions.

I have to make many decisions,
If I kill them I'll be stuck like that for life.
My fear is rising
I'm stuck in amnesia, all alone
I'm lost, lost in my head.

They don't care what pain they gave me,
And now, I shall cause,
Suffering, pain, misery and hatred,
Their minds will be corrupted,
To avenge my father will make me calm,
But at the moment,
I'm lost, lost in my dreams.

But not to worry,
For in time I shall grow stronger,
He has kept me in containment for so long now,
He will learn.
Since I will put a new phrase in the dictionary,
Power has a new name,
Fear!

Navneet Kandhari (11)
Wallington County Grammar School

Becoming A Hero

I want to be a hero,
With my power and courage,
I will be ready for any obstacles that come in my way,
I will be brave, destructive and determined to take on anyone.

I want to be a hero,
And I will demolish anything that comes in my way,
I will be helpful to people that are on my side,
I will avenge my friends' deaths with their killers' deaths.

I want to be a hero,
That is full of strength,
And I want to be rapid so I can chase anyone down,
I am full of hatred, as I hate my friends' killers,
I will hunt them down and kill them like they killed my friends.

I want to be a hero,
As from now I am a hero,
I will get the people that killed my friends when I see them,
I will take them on one by one and I will kill them,
I have witnessed a lot of deaths,
And now I will commit *deaths*.

Dhruvesh Desai (11)
Wallington County Grammar School

Lost

My head rang like a church bell
All the thoughts of my head were spinning
Like a whirlwind of quotes and phrases
I was stuck in a world where you had
To fight to stay alive

Life felt like a never-ending journey
For food and shelter
I was as deserted as a wolf without its pack
Life felt as though it was drifting away
I was truly lost
Lost in a place, different from any other.

George Webster (11)
Wallington County Grammar School

Battle

I lie here in no-man's-land.
I can hear our armies being worn down
Because of the rapid attacks
From the other armies.

They bring with them death and destruction
And all things of the Devil.
Their cellophane slugs and gum balls,
They bring with them deepest sorrow.

Here they come again with auto death.
Why do they forever torment us?
We live a life of torture,
In pain and fear of them.

There are children in the villages they destroy.
Why has the almighty punished us so?
All we can do is fight endlessly,
Fight and die.

When I die, which I will,
At least I will be remembered by the world.
As one of the people who fought,
Fought against them.

Iain Milne (11)
Wallington County Grammar School

Hallowe'en

The werewolves will come and give you a fright,
At 12 o'clock in the dim moonlight.
The monsters will come and give you a scare,
With razor-sharp teeth and locks of green hair.
Spiders will come and make you jump
And you'll fall back to Earth with a great big *bump!*
Bats will come and make you scream
And then you'll wake up and find it's a dream!

Ben Elliott (11)
Wallington County Grammar School

War-Torn

Cold light of dawn, penetrated walls of hope
Remnants of survival littered the battle zone
Pillars of hope
Remained only to be engulfed by dark waves of apprehension
Solid footsteps
Echoed in silence
Unanswered world around
Dead
Ghosts emerged from their haunted houses
Gaunt faces smiled superficially
And the routine started again
Children played but war groped in their shadows
Legacy buried under mounds of death
Granda's pipe burned tobacco no more
In one day the window of sanity came crashing down
Children cried waterfalls of tears
Trains arrived
Children piled on
Spitfires whizzed overhead proud like eagles
Teary eyes gaze drearily
For some new life, new chance, but for others damage is permanent.

Harry Wrightson (13)
Wallington County Grammar School

Centurion Tank

Centurion tank, metal and shiny, caterpillar tracks
churning the earth.

Centurion tank, proud and brave, armour and
gun barrel gleaming.

Centurion tank, sounds like thunder, makes
the earth shudder!

Alex Purcell (12)
Wallington County Grammar School

Why Me?

Why is it always me?
When I'm falling apart.
Breaking into pieces all the time.
I never seem to get out of things,
When I'm trapped inside.
There's just nowhere to go, nowhere to hide.

Why is it always me getting
Beaten up at school?
Being distracted from lessons,
My shirt now stained with blood.
Then knowing that I have to endure,
This is all at home.

I try to explain,
But it doesn't get through to you.
Every time you seem to ignore me,
But I still talk on like I don't notice anything wrong
And I know it won't change.

Why me?
Why me?

Anthony Daniel (13)
Wallington County Grammar School

A Twister

It is a high speed spinning top,
It is a howling wolf in a vicious storm,
It is a corkscrew digging in the ground,
It is a toddler in destructive mode,
It is a big grey monster,
It is a master of disaster,
It is a natural but cruel phenomenon,
It is a mini hurricane but with more power,
It is a very scary nightmare,
It is a careless freak of nature!

Jared Sweeney (11)
Wallington County Grammar School

Ode To A Poet

I'm finding it hard to make a rhyme,
To get the words to fit the line,
Words come easily to mind
But the right order I can't find!
Written down it's so confusing,
All sense and meaning it is losing.

One idea seems so right,
So I work all through the night,
Then I find, come the day,
I have to throw it all away!
I'm getting really stressed,
How I try to do my best.

Being Wordsworth's such a curse,
I have to perfect every verse.

Timothy McKavanagh (12)
Wallington County Grammar School

Injustice

Why do people starve, when others have too much food to eat?
Why do people murder the harmless?
Why is a group punished because of one individual
And why are there so many homeless?

Why is a race condemned, because of a false stereotype?
Why does a country fall to ruin, because of one wrong decision?
And why do people go poor, when
Some have so much money they lose it?

How can there be so much injustice,
So much unfairness?
Why is the world so corrupt
And when will it stop?

Only God knows.

Adam Gye (13)
Wallington County Grammar School

Poem Of Life

Through the air,
His soul floats.
To the skies
And heavens it goes,
How it happened,
No one knows
Last time they saw him,
Was in the woods.
Yet his body now lays quite still,
His pulse tranquil.
Heart stopped
And his body cropped.
His mind was peaceful,
Closed were his eyes,
Never again will he arise.

But through his death,
A war will end.
A great nation,
A great country,
Will rise again.
'Twas thousands of lives,
This devil has snatched.
But now they can,
Rest in peace.

Mohammed Kaba (12)
Wallington County Grammar School

The Dinosaur

Its dark eyes filled its face
Its raging legs moved at a pace
Its sharp claws ripping the air
The dinosaur killed without a care.

Sam Hanson (11)
Wallington County Grammar School

Camp Green Lake

There's no lake at Camp Green Lake
Camp Green Lake used to be the largest lake in Texas
But that was over 100 years ago
Now it's just a dry, flat wasteland
In the day it is 95 degrees in the shade
If you can find any shade
There are only two old oak trees
There's a hammock between the two oak trees
Behind that a log cabin stands
There are scorpions and rattlesnakes on the lake
They won't bother you if you don't bother them
Usually!
That's nothing compared to the yellow spotted lizard
If you are bitten you will die slowly and painfully
Always!

Meekaaeel Valimohamed (11)
Wallington County Grammar School

Wonders Of The Stars

The stars shine in the sky so shiny and bright,
I would go up to count them if I wasn't afraid of heights.
I tried to count them but it was confusing and hard,
One tiny star is better than one million gold shards.

I look through my telescope every night and see the planets sleeping,
When I first saw this sight it sent me weeping.
I believe I've touched the stars, they were in the palm of my hand,
The stars began to jump up and down and crawl on my
                              make poverty history band.

The feel of the stars is amazing, I feel warm inside, when
                              my mum comes in,
The stars go off and hide.
When it's time for bed,
The stars stay on my pillow and run around my head.

Ajay Rose (11)
Wallington County Grammar School

Escape!

He was in, what now?
He gripped the gear lever,
D for drive,
The truck flung forward
He pushed the pedal to the floor,
Boof!
Over a pile of dirt
He was in mid-air now
The bonnet of the vehicle dropped downwards
He was going to land straight into a hole,
Boof!
An airbag flew out of the steering wheel
Quickly he leaped out of the side door
Ran
He ran like he'd never ran before!

Joe Stanek (11)
Wallington County Grammar School

The Yellow Spotted Lizard!

The horrible fear
The piercing red eyes
The swift tongue
The razor black teeth
The eleven yellow spots
One wrong move and . . .
Wham!
You're going to die
Slowly, painfully
And suffering beyond belief
Don't bother
The monster
The killer
The terrifying
Yellow spotted lizard!

Joseph Field (11)
Wallington County Grammar School

The Match

Lively atmosphere
Roaring crowd
Enthusiastic players
A manager proud

Smashing hits
Scorching goals
Beautiful saves
Rattling off football posts
Lovely passes, drifting crosses
Dashing runs
So many chances

The cup is shining
It is either win or lose
The players are trying
It's like you're on a cruise

At last there is a winner
Happy faces everywhere
Congratulating each other
The losers can do nothing but stare

The cup is given
The winners cheer
After, they open a bottle
And out comes beer

At the end of the day
Everyone is a winner
When it comes to the match
No one is a loser.

Eeruj Shaikh (11)
Wallington County Grammar School

Holes

(Based on the book 'Holes' by Louis Sachar)

A pair of old sneakers
Supposedly fell from the sky
Hit Stanley on the head
While he was walking on by

He picked them up from the ground
Looked up, looked down, right then left
A police siren began to ring
'The shoes found me it couldn't be theft'

As the car emerged, the sound grew louder
He glanced at the spot he picked
And he ran and he ran and he ran and he ran
Stanley knew he was about to be nicked

As the judge asked him a question in court
'How did you find these shoes?'
Stanley told the story but nobody believed him
But he knew it was definitely true

The judge had made his conclusion
To jail or Camp Green Lake
Stanley considered his options and chose
If only he knew it was a mistake

Off to Camp Green Lake he went
The ride being bumpy and hot
He desperately needed a drink or three
Whether it was clean or not.

Gregory Clare (11)
Wallington County Grammar School

The Lizards

Stanley tried and tried
His and Zero's tunnel was
Deeper and wider

Suddenly they touched
A hard and solid object
They pulled it out
It was a suitcase

A beam of light came
Over Stanley and Zero
Suddenly some creatures
Leaped towards them

They were several deadly
Yellow spotted lizards

The eyes of the lizards
Which were sparkling
Were staring into
Stanley and Zero's eyes

They smelt the lizards'
Putrid breath
As they crawled
Around them

Mouths open the lizards
Are ready to kill.

David Liao (11)
Wallington County Grammar School

Chicken On A Plate

A piece of chicken on a plate
Waiting for me and my date
I don't think that I really can wait
She's probably going to be late.

Jonathan Lee-Akinbile (12)
Wallington County Grammar School

Run Away?

(Inspired by the book 'Holes' by Louis Sachar)

'What do you see?'
Said Mr Sir.
'Not much,'
Stanley replied.
'Any guard towers?'
'No.'
'Electric fence,
Any fence?'
'No, nothing.'
'You could run away.'

Mr Sir had a gun,
Stanley looked at it.
'I'm not going to shoot you,'
Mr Sir assured him.
'You can just run away.'
'No,'
Stanley said.
His reply was,
'Good,
It's impossible.'

George Hutchins (12)
Wallington County Grammar School

Dust

Dust has such a boring life,
Floating around through space.
It does nothing else, just flies around
And rests on top of a cupboard.

Dust just annoys everyone,
Getting in their way.
They spend their money on a dust wipe
And the dust just floats back down again!

James Luke Wellsted (11)
Wallington County Grammar School

Yellow Spotted Lizard

Y ellow spots
E vil red eyes
L icking up the blood
L oving every drop
O nion hater
W ild and dangerous

S piteful in every way
P reying on its victim
O pposing threat
T arantula eater
T errifying
E choing screams
D eath will come before you

L ying in wait
I ce-cold stare
Z ombie-like features
A ims to kill
R uthless with its teeth
D ead.

Daniel Clancy (11)
Wallington County Grammar School

Hallowe'en

H airy spiders everywhere
A ngry monsters coming to get you
L eeches sucking your blood
L ocusts flying at you
O wls howling at moonlight
W itches with broomsticks and wolves looking for prey
E erie and dark feelings in everybody's minds
E verybody is scared
N ever enter the Devil's lair.

Christian Eede (11)
Wallington County Grammar School

Shadow Man

The shadow man follows me

Black as night,
He follows me,
Light as a feather,
He follows me,

He goes at night.

When morning breaks,
He follows me,
When I'm at school,
He follows me,
Like a best friend,
Wrapping his invisible arms around me,
Keeping me safe.

He stops when I'm grown and leave
And I say,
'Thanks for being there Dad.'

Matthew Avis (11)
Wallington County Grammar School

Love

Love is something that happens to all
To people tall or small.
Love is something that lasts for life
Gifts and cards show it all.
Love is something of a game
Competing against others who like the same.
Love is something which keeps you thinking
So your heart won't start sinking.
Love is something like a dream
One day it might become true.
Love is something you should cherish
You never know, you might one day perish.
No matter how old or young
Love is something that will stay strong.

Umar Ghulab (12)
Wallington County Grammar School

Mysterious Sneakers

A pair of sneakers,
Falling from the sky
One hit him on the head,
He wondered whose they were.

What should he do?
He ran and ran,
He heard the sirens,
And didn't know what to do.

It was like a sign,
Like a gift from God,
From his dad the inventor,
Who recycled old shoes.

The policeman got out,
Asking Stanley questions,
'Why are you running?
Where did you get those shoes?'

Sajjidali Alidina (11)
Wallington County Grammar School

Green Lake

(Inspired by the book 'Holes' by Louis Sachar)

G reen is a rare sight at Camp Green Lake
R ed eyes stare at you from holes
E ven the lizards stay in the shade
E ating in the shade
N o one knows the truth about the place

L akes are filled with water but not this one
A rid desert as far as the eye can see
K ids dig the holes
E vil eyes watch them.

Benjamin David Cook (11)
Wallington County Grammar School

A Wolf Tale

I am a wolf,
Noble and kind.
I travel in a pack,
Never leaving them behind.

We trek deep into the forest,
Creeping swiftly and silent.
Pouncing on our prey,
Hunting until twilight.

Then we rest,
But before we can sleep we hear footsteps,
Coming closer and closer.
The whole pack runs, survival of the fittest.

We just keep running,
No matter what.
But suddenly we are trapped by a pack . . .
Humans! And *bang!* I am dead,
Asleep in my lifeless bed.

We can't keep killing,
Using lives like toys.
Breaking them and then disposing of them.
But one day we will be the toys,
Being shot, dead,
Sleeping in our lifeless beds.

Seth Scafe-Smith (11)
Wallington County Grammar School

The Yellow Spotted Lizard

The yellow spotted lizard is a fierce beast.
As soon as it bites you you're a buzzard feast.

Its deadly venom is purple and cold.
Although it will not bite if onion you hold.

It doesn't matter if you're ten or twenty-four.
As soon as it bites you, you shall live no more.

Henry Miller (11)
Wallington County Grammar School

My Eden

I gaze down upon the dazzling beauty of Rome,
My Eden.
The temples grander than the gods of Olympus.
My heaven.
With Seraphims in armour.
Only a person like a god could do this.
Me, Julius Caesar.

I stare through a hole at the destroyed remains of Rome.
The temples crumbling like fallen Titans.
Roman soldiers pierced with spears and crushed with axes
And worst of all,
Barbarians charging down anything in their path,
Razing everything to the ground.
While I, Julius Caesar, gaze on Rome.
My Eden.

Daniel Willmott (11)
Wallington County Grammar School

Guess

I'm heard but not seen,
If I'm white I'm good,
Children use me and adults too,
I'm the easy way out,
Used too much and I'll be found out,
I can get you places you have dreamed,
I can make your life hell,
I'm being told all over the world,
Every second,
Trying to keep me from being discovered;
Is the most difficult thing,
Do you know what I am?
I'm lies.

Emilio Sullivan (12)
Wallington County Grammar School

My Inner Voices

'Go ahead
Hit him back,
You're bigger,' she said.

Should I . . .
Teach the bully a lesson,
Punch him in the gut,
Kick him in his shins,
Pull his hair,
Poke out his eyes,
Squeeze his neck . . .
And get into trouble.

Or . . .
Walk away,
Do nothing,
More like do something,
Tell a teacher,
Get his parents in,
Tell them what their son has done
And get the job finished.

What do you think?

Jack Rawbone (11)
Wallington County Grammar School

World War Chav

My name is Chas
I am a chav
Saying to people no money I have
Two sisters I have
They are Sweater and Bhav
I listen to rhythm and blues
Don't have no money to buy shoes
So my motto is: what have I to lose?

Michael Anaman (13)
Wallington County Grammar School

The Race

My heart was beating,
Sweat trickling down my face,
A bullet fired,
Fear shot through my body,
It had started,
I longed for my mother's words,
Reassuring and calm,
Anxious faces staring,
What should I do?
My legs began to pump,
I saw my mother in the stands,
I felt a surge of renewed energy,
Flowing through my veins,
One boy was ahead,
My legs pumped harder,
People were cheering me,
I had won!

Oliver Rodin (11)
Wallington County Grammar School

Tiger, Tiger

(Inspired by 'Tyger' by William Blake)

Tiger! Tiger! Burning bright
In the forest of the night
Waiting for its prey
Ready to pounce every day

Tiger! Tiger! Burning bright
With great force and might
Eyes, fiery red
Waiting to make something dead

Tiger! Tiger! Burning bright
In the forest of the night
Waiting for its prey
Ready to pounce every day.

Michael Sowole (12)
Wallington County Grammar School

Yellow Spotted Lizard

Y earning for a new victim
E vil red-eyed lizard
L eaping monster
L apping up the blood
O nion hater
W ounding others

S pringing into action
P utting a capital F in fear
O pening its frill
T errifying creature
T errible in every way
E liminating stare
D eadly and dangerous

L eaves the body and becomes buzzard food
I guanas and chameleons share the same family
Z ooming eyes like a camera
A iming for the fatal blow
R esting on its spot (patiently waiting)
D iving for the kill.

Niral Mehta (12)
Wallington County Grammar School

The World Of Food

Whether it's junk like pizza, burgers or cake,
Or stuff that is good for you like apples, salads or tuna steak,
It's all food,
When you eat you should never be rude.
There are billions of meals to choose from,
Like beans with chips and a chicken goujon.
There is food that swims like fish
And food that is served in a dish,
There is food that is fast
And food that is always served last,
This is all because the world of food is vast.

Tor Abrams (11)
Wallington County Grammar School

My Holes Poem

(Inspired by the book 'Holes' by Louis Sachar)

The venomous scar on his face
Glinting in the early morning moonlight
He stood at the oatmeal pot
His filthy scraggly hands holding the whimpering camper
As he thought of what evil punishment to give to him
All the camper could do was to stare right into his eyes

Stanley was half awake when he was in the breakfast line
But the sight of the camper and Mr Sir's scar awakened him
Mr Sir threw the boy to an adjacent pot
He then asked the camp if there was anything wrong with his face
The boys didn't dare to say a word

Mr Sir went back to his job with the repulsive oatmeal
Stanley was next in the line
He wondered what Mr Sir would do to him as he apprehensively
                                    walked towards him
The cold air rushed through the wooden doors of the canteen
                                    and around Stanley.

Dominic Simon George Powell (11)
Wallington County Grammar School

The Lost Soul Of The Knight

He withers in the dark sky
But he is very shy
To show his appearance to male or female

His eyes like fire
His nose like a pecker
He is the dark soul of the knight

Day by day, night by night
He is the only one true knight
He watches man and woman by broad daylight.

Yannick Li Tai Leong (12)
Wallington County Grammar School

The Long Walk

Open, dry plain,
No life I can see,
I may be buzzard food,
But it feels good to be free.

Huge, deserted plain,
Which way should I go?
Should I go back?
This could be Ground Zero.

Humid, hot plain,
Has God forsaken me?
Nowhere to go,
No one to set me free.

Silent, dead plain,
No life I can see,
Should I go back?
Is this the end for me?

Ilyas Morrison (11)
Wallington County Grammar School

Greenlake Camp

(Inspired by the book 'Holes' by Louis Sachar)

  G enerating heat far too quickly
  R avenous thirst while I wait for the truck
  E nergy draining like a sewer
yE llow spotted lizards to be aware
  N ot what I expected
  L ittle time to myself
  A ll I do is dig holes
  K nowing each day one hole: 5' deep 5' wide
  E veryone has their hopes up

'C arry the clouds over the mountains!'
 A ll of the clouds stay there frozen
 M any of the clouds filled with rain
'P our on us and get rid of our misery . . . please!'

Robert Lewis Oman (11)
Wallington County Grammar School

My Perfect Score

I looked at my math sheet
I was very amazed
The whole class looked at me
Whilst I sat there just dazed.

The teacher approached me
With a very big frown
His face was not smiling
Whilst I looked down.

The class went silent
You could hear my heart beat
A pin dropped on the floor
I was *dead meat!*

'This is not a good score,' he yelled in my ear
I looked at the paper
I was feeling headstrong
It then occurred to me what had gone wrong!

This can't be right, I thought to myself
I had practised all week to get them all right
The explanation was then plain to see
The paper did not belong to me.

I frowned at the teacher who stood there dazed
I hadn't got them wrong, I was amazed
The other Joe Turner should be in my shoes
This was guaranteed to be headline news!

Joe Turner (11)
Wallington County Grammar School

The Age Of Man

Life is a maze, one giant maze;
It has many entrances but no way out,
Just one goal in the centre . . .
First a stranger, vomiting, crying, lost.
He crawls around on his hands and knees,
He makes it round the first ring of the maze;
But has arrived at many dead ends.
In the second stage he can walk,
Almost talk; he is a cute young boy
But is still lost in the giant maze of life.
Then the young school boy,
Reluctantly creeping to school
With his giant bag on his back.
Next the teenager,
Skateboarding along listening to loud music,
Waking up at 11am after a long night of clubbing.
Then the adult, he is a grown man now,
He's made it this far he can't give up.
The sixth stage is a worker,
He's promoted and earning money; lots of it.
Then a retired man,
He is wise and noble,
He has a simple life living off pensions.
Afterwards an old and feeble man
Sitting in his rocking chair.
And finally after a long life
He has reached his final goal,
He's made it round the maze of life.

Adam Taylor (12)
Wallington County Grammar School

The Eagle

Casts a shadow on the ground
Soars through the sea above the sea
Slowly sinking to the ground
As would a rock in water
Vigilance is thy name, bird of prey

Perched on an arm of the mountain
The pools of black, so deep and endless
Reflected in them
The shadows of the years gone by

Talons sharp as knives
Gleaming in dawn's light
The stain of death marks their cruelty
They hang below, as does their importance
They are not like the worn down dagger above
For without this dagger the being does not exist

This is the eagle wrapped in nature's coat
Which prowls the skies
As a shark would in the sea
Endless is its journey
But it may rest for another day.

Peter Wotherspoon (11)
Wallington County Grammar School

Animals

They point at me like the gorilla in the next cage,
Mouth open all the time smacking the glass,
Zookeepers hold back their rampage,
Like they're better than me.

The tiger in the next cage looks angry,
'Already,' said my friend on the tyre above,
What an animal, I don't mean to sound lairy,
No worry the other animals laugh at us anyway.

Edward Butler (12)
Wallington County Grammar School

Do You Want My Gun?

Do you want my gun, or do you want my life?
Do you want my gun, or do you want my wife?
Do you want my gun, or do you want my store?
Do you want just my gun, or much, much more?

What is it you really want? I must ask myself,
For it is one of the few freedoms we have left.
Maybe it's something more political you seek,
But can't accomplish unless we become weak.

When people can no longer defend their rights,
Their days become filled with sleepless nights,
And soon their fears become much, much more,
When the secret police knock at their door.

They took them from their family, and their home,
And without trial they locked them up alone.
No visitors, no place they could appeal,
For they were politically incorrect to party zeal.

Today the majority of us are not 'politically correct'.
And what do the liberals want us to put in check?
That's right, our guns, they want us to turn them in.
As long as we have guns socialism cannot win!

Each day this Howard thing denies our rights,
As he puts God-loving people in his sights.
I will keep my gun, I'll use it if I must,
To defend my right to say 'In God I trust!'

The foundation of this land of ours,
Is now being threatened, and it may only be hours,
Until God is completely removed from every part,
And this country is stripped of its very heart!

Today freedom is no longer a 'right',
It's a battleground for which we must fight.
So if you ask me for my gun . . . the answer is . . . *no!*
Try to take it and if there is a Hell, you'll know.

Christopher Jackson (13)
Wallington County Grammar School

When I'm Old

When I'm old and cannot see,
I shan't wait for the death of me
I'll cruise the world on an ocean liner
Or be the diner of a restaurant finer.
I'll do my hair in a very droll way
An afro, as some might say.
But there's no chance of stopping there
I'll spend my cash on designer chairs
Or walk the streets in an eager mood
To try and find expensive food.
Fish eggs can be doubted not
But oysters really hit the spot!

But what to do if I tire of that?
I can't be pleased by meagre chat
I'll want a more exciting adventure
To the densest jungle I'll venture.
I'll laugh at tigers and spit on crocs,
No one can beat me, I'm the tops.
But soon, not that it will suit my need
I'll need new prey on which to feed.
Ah! the watchers of a theatre play!
I'll run and jump and dance all day!

But no, I don't think I'll do that really.
It's not too good for me, sincerely.
'Cause it'll crack my every bone,
I think I prefer it back at home.

Gabriel Nicklin (12)
Wallington County Grammar School

Dracula: A Poem About Lucy!

Once day Lucy got a visit,
It was her sister Mina.
Mina was yet to discover,
Lucy had three proposals.
First there was John Seward,
At an age of
Merely twenty-nine.
On the other hand,
He was the boss of a large asylum,
Yet still she turned him down.
Poor Dr Seward,
Was left as a measly friend.
Then there came another,
Quincy Morris.
An American man,
Who travelled a lot.
But one evening he surprised Lucy,
With an unexpected proposal,
But Lucy's heart was for someone else.
Arthur Holmwood was the one,
He had won Lucy's heart.
He had to go to his father,
As he was unwell,
But soon he would return to marry Lucy.
Not long after,
Dracula bit into Lucy's neck.
Lucy then became evil,
Until Arthur drove the wooden stake
Right into Lucy's heart.

George Hall (12)
Wallington County Grammar School

Untitled

As poor as a church mouse
As cunning as a fox
As swift as a hawk
As thick as *thieves!*

As heavy as an elephant
As brave as a lion
As mad as a hotter
As frisky as a lamb
Wrestlers!

As happy as a child
As graceful as a swan
As happy as a lark
As gentle as a lamb
Babies!

As loyal as an apostle
As fierce as a lion
As playful as a puppy
As agile as a monkey
Dogs!

As obstinate as a mule
As pleased as punch
As alike as two herrings
As devoted as a mother
Parents!

Jaspreet Singh Manoor (12)
Wallington County Grammar School

Lunch On A Saturday

All lovely and warm
Crunchy and crisp
Or smooth and succulent
Soft mashed potato
Or crisp waffles
Juicy tomato
Or crunchy apples
Smooth chicken
Tasty sausage
It's so hard to choose!

Burgers and chips
Or maybe . . .
Jacket potato and cheese
For dessert I fancy
Strawberries and cream
Not too creamy
Maybe ice-cold ice cream
I had it last week
So hard to choose
Are crisps too original?
Lovely pizza
Dreamy cream
I love lunch on a . . . *Saturday.*

Daniel Josiah Hawthorne (11)
Wallington County Grammar School

Sandwich Fillings

Ham, spam, cheese or jam,
Bacon, sausage or crisp,
Marmite is yummy,
But tuna is scrummy,
Is there anything that I've missed?

In white bread,
Brown bread,
Or a ciabatta roll,
Make it taste pleasant and nice,
Make it good for your soul!

Mayonnaise or salad cream,
Tomato sauce - it'll make you scream.
For this sandwich will go far,
Further than a shooting star,
Oh yes this sandwich will go far!

Matthew Blow (11)
Wallington County Grammar School

Machine Gunners

Chas was a young boy,
Who was smashed and bashed by Boddser like a toy.

Then Chas had found a gun,
With it he thought he'd have great fun.

But along with the gun came disaster,
Bruises and cuts that needed a plaster.

Along with the gun came danger,
Rudi, a friend or a stranger?

Chas and his friends had built a greater bond,
Now with Rudi in the scenes, of him they were quite fond.

Finally the story comes to an end,
Quite fond of Rudi, they lose a good friend.

Imran Butt (12)
Wallington County Grammar School

The Tiger

He creeps through the autumn grasses,
    Prowling, crawling
The rain soaks his fur coat,
    Howling, blowing
He stops, on his hind legs,
    Watching, glaring
His legs start to move again,
    Faster, faster
His feet squat behind him,
    Ready to . . .
    Pounce!
He lies on the dusty ground,
    Yawning, lazily
Scratching an old, dead tree,
    Slowly, sleepily
His teeth drip with deer blood,
    As he stretches out, sleeping.

Jonathan Mayo (12)
Wallington County Grammar School

The Snow Last Week

All last week I saw the snow fall,
Once last week I threw a snowball.
The snow in my hand gleamed pearly-white,
I threw my snowball with all my might.
My big white snowball span
And opposition ran.
My big white snowball flew across the yard
And hit my brother very hard.
My brother fell down,
Gave me a hard frown.
He rushed inside quick and told my mother,
I tried to explain; she said, 'Don't bother.'

Abdulrahman El-Hilly (12)
Wallington County Grammar School

A Day In The Life Of A Secondary School Kid

I wake up at 6.30am, to see the blinding sun,
I get off my bed and hear my brother laughing,
I don't know why he is having a laugh, it isn't much fun.

I walk down the stairs only half awake,
I see food and pounce like a lion,
It's toast, at least give me cereal for God's sake.

I go up stairs to brush my teeth and wash my face,
I have my brother and sisters banging on the door,
At least now I don't have my mom on my case.

I enter my room and start to change,
I hear my mom shout, 'Quickly, you've got five minutes!'
When I've finished I say, 'I hate these clothes,
They make me look strange.'

I'm at the stop, it's pouring rain,
I haven't got a coat or an umbrella,
I should have brought either, it would have been a gain.

I'm at school now, I feel in depression,
Especially when I get to geography,
I didn't complete my homework, now I've got a detention.

School is finally over, what a relief,
But now I've got the bus ride home,
It's as hard as eating beef.

I return home feeling berserk,
I had a fight at school
And now I've got homework.

Ghalib Zaidi (13)
Wallington County Grammar School

The Thing Of The Night

Its menacing yellow eyes were glowing against the starry sky
Like glow-in-the-dark vampire teeth, only an evil yellow.
The glare paralysed me, sending cold shocks through my body,
A truly frightening sight to behold.

Its teeth were sharper than knives,
They were as shiny as polished silver.
Blood and saliva dripped from its mouth to the floor,
Its breath was hot and smelled of the blood of its victims.

It had a muscular frame, its arms and legs like tree trunks.
Wings with razor-sharp edges and a hairy tail were sprouted from
its back.
It had hairs the colour of soil and claws which still contained
the flesh of victims.
All of this and towering over me at seven feet tall.

It suddenly charged towards me, I had nowhere to run.
I dived out of the path of the beast and made a bold dash
in one random direction.
The thing smashed its horned head into a tree and fell unconscious.
Under the cover of the night, I crawled through the grass
of the field, my heart about to explode.

I was convinced I was safe, got up and walked around,
Back in the familiar area of my local park.
I headed home, but I turned into my road and was
surrounded by more of the vile things,
But a ray of sunlight came through, rebounded off a car mirror
and struck each of the things.
A mighty roar came through from each of them and they melted
into the sky at dawn.

Ishan De Silva (12)
Wallington County Grammar School

Drugs Are Bad

Don't take drugs they are very bad
When you take them you'll go mad
You will be punished by your dad
Also it will make your mama sad

After a while you'll go insane
And then when you're driving you'll be in the wrong lane
You might forget to shave and grow a big mane
And then you have no hope of going sane

Drugs are a way of escaping the problems of life
You may go mental with a big knife
And soon you'll have no wife
And then you have ruined your life

When you get caught by the police what will you do?
You won't be able to sue
And you'll have no one to turn to
They make you go mad and this is what drugs do

You flap into a trap when you take them
And when you're caught the police will give you your own den
And you'll be locked up with many silly men
And then you wish you'd never taken them

Now you're not looking so sly
And now all you can do is sigh
Every day you wish you never told a lie
And now every day you just wait till you die

Only fools take drugs
It makes them turn into thugs
So never take them
Or you will be one of them.

Tahir Shivji (12)
Wallington County Grammar School

Howzat!

Lords is buzzing
The time is here, to make your test debut
Against a team to fear
The Aussies, the mighty, mighty Aussies

13-2, in at number 4
Up steps Warne, the great Shane Warne
It will be a ripper you say, no a slider - he's bowled,
It hits you on the pad, *'Howzat,'* he shouts! Plum LBW 'No,'
says Koertzen

'He's fishing there, Warner,' shouts Gilchrist
'Howzat!'
'No,' says Koertzen
'Howzat!'
'No,' says Koertzen
'Howzat!'
'No,' says Koertzen

An over passes; you're stuck with Warney
'Howzat!'
'No,' says Koertzen
'Howzat!;
'No,' says Koertzen
'Give it a rest.'
'No,' says Warner.

You're 13-2, you're stuck with Warner
'Howzat!'
'No,' says Koertzen
'Howzat!'
No,' says Koertzen
'Howz-'
'Six,' says Scola.

Matthew Scola   (13)
Wallington County Grammar School

Sport

There once was a footballer called Scholes,
Who used to score lots of great goals.
But now he's too old
And needs to be sold,
Before all he's good for is bowls.

A tennis player called Henman,
Said he could take on ten men.
He practised all day,
Until light faded away,
But was shattered so he couldn't play them.

There once was a hurdler called Jackson,
He was always first off at the klaxon.
But one day in training,
It started raining
And all of them had to put macs on!

Andrew James (12)
Wallington County Grammar School

The Sea

Sea, sea! Oh mighty sea!
I call for thee, I call for thee!
I hear you moaning
I hear you groaning.
Please don't be angry with me.

Sea, sea! Oh mighty sea!
I call for thee, I call for thee!
I hear you crying
I hear you whining
Please, oh please don't be angry with me.

Sea, sea! Oh mighty sea!
I look away from what I see
I see you laughing
I see you smirking
But I'm not, I never will be.

Rohit Sood (12)
Wallington County Grammar School

The Man Of Iron

The man of iron bold and brave
Through the fire from where he came,
Battered and bruised
Annoyed and enraged.

Made from the souls of Hell
Conjured up into a spell,
It formed, twisted and twined
Until the muscle hath finally arrived.

The man of iron bold and brave
From the fire from where he came,
Merciless and cold
With no feeling of looking old.

It looks like a putrid mess
Looking for victims to obliterate,
It looks high and low
Never minds the trees swaying to and fro.

The man of iron bold and brave
Back into the fire from where he came
Never to return again.

Fareed Fletcher-Lord (12)
Wallington County Grammar School

The Cat

A playful life
So cute and strong
A doubled life
Of killing and kindness

A child's heart
A warrior's spirit
Nine lives
Brought into one.

Matthew Murrell (12)
Wallington County Grammar School

The Tiger

They lurk in the shadows,
Ready to strike.
Breezing across the African plain throughout the night.
They're all around, ready to bite
So beware the tigers' strike.

Their dangerous strike is full of might
It will swipe and frighten you.
Nothing is more powerful than a tiger's strike.
They have the brains, they have the might,
A tiger is a perfect animal with a perfect life.

Watch them hunt, see them run,
They can take you down any day.
With their tigers' strike,
It will swipe you and frighten you.

They're full of hunger,
They're full of fright,
Never merciful,
Never quite know when they'll bite.
But one thing is for sure,
They're a beautiful sight.

Aravind Mootien (12)
Wallington County Grammar School

The Fortress

There stood the fortress big and tall
Towering over them all
The soldiers inside tall and stark
Almost invisible in the dark
The cellars full of ammunition
Upstairs they worry about munitions
Soldiers of every kind
But only one thing in mind.

Amal Vaidya (12)
Wallington County Grammar School

Money

I have come to the end,

My life is now over,
So much for the four-leaved clover.

My life has wondered astray,
If only I had changed my betting way.

I gambled it all,
I have been such a fool,
I just look at rich people,
I sit and drool.

The tables have now turned,
All I've ever earned,
Has been put down as a wager,
Won all the little things, nothing major.

Until one day,
When I lost all of my life,
Including the house, my kids and even my wife.

Shane Freemantle (12)
Wallington County Grammar School

Think!

All the people, that are cold and wet.
All the people that are lonely and sad.
All the people that have no comfort or friends.
All the people that have nowhere to go.
All the people that are living off nothing.
Think of them, think of you.
So when you think (I'm bored, I want, I wish I had,
I need, I can't, I don't want to, I won't.)
Just think of them and think of you.
Remember this, and think how lucky you are.
Think of you and think of them.
Think.

Hugh Macdonald (13)
Wallington County Grammar School

My World

Lumpy beds and doing chores,
Drama lessons and rugby games.
These are the things I hate.

Action-packed books and football games,
Comedy shows and talking to my mates.
These are the things I love.

Science lessons and old cars,
The smell of cigarettes and gone-off milk.
These are the things I hate.

Listening to music and swimming in the sea,
Eating Mexican and sleeping in.
These are the things I love.

I love many things and hate many too.
But I wouldn't like to change them because . . .
I simply love my world.

Ben Richardson (12)
Wallington County Grammar School

Moods

My colleague broke me
I aimed to hit him abominably
What mood is that?
It's anger

Tears discharge from your eyes
It makes you announce countless lies
What mood is that?
It's sadness

It makes you cheerful
Never makes you dull
What mood is that?
It's happiness.

Nirojan Jesuthasan (12)
Wallington County Grammar School

I Remember Those Days

I remember those dreary days
When black people were slaves

Our ancestors had scars on their backs
Racially abused because they were black

A long time ago, we used to live in home-made shacks
Now even in the Third World, the poverty has come back

I remember black people trembling with fear
All my black people shedding more than one tear

When Martin Luther King was shot in the chest
Back in those days we did not have Teflon vests

During this rough time we discovered soul
Almost a century ago, when we were in mines for coal

But now and today after these hard times we have persevered
Now many a black father can provide for his kids and his dear

This question is so sad that everybody could cry
Why did these innocent people die?

I don't know why I ask this question
All people should get on with people with love and affection.

Theodore Davis (12)
Wallington County Grammar School

As Free As A Bird

Over the edge I dived,
The wind caught my face;
I felt alive.
As free as a bird
Not a sound could be heard
As I hovered up high
In the big blue sky.,
As I hovered, up high,
In the big blue sky.

Harry Pike (12)
Wallington County Grammar School

Gangsters

All gangsters carry a gun,
When they shoot someone they know they've got to run.
If they see someone they just shoot,
Empty the clip and put the body in the boot.

They walk around with their AKs and their shanks,
The more people they kill, the higher their rank.
Not even giving it a second thought,
Until they rip and then get caught.

Now they're locked up in jail,
With every day police checking their mail.
Few weeks pass and the next thing in the post,
Is a kilo of weed from the east coast.

But now these gangsters are getting out of control,
We need more police to be on patrol,
People like Tupac and 50 getting shot,
Some survive, however some may not.

Benjamin Donelien (12)
Wallington County Grammar School

War

Bullets flying everywhere,
People sweating here and there,
Will we win? That's the question.
The enemy says, *'No!'*
Yes we say, however, as we speak more and more of us are dying,
The flames are burning us all to death,
But then the bombers come and . . . *bang!*
Death has come to us all except a few.
Cadavers carpet the floor.
Our families feel hopeless,
Is the trauma worth it?

Sam Clark (12)
Wallington County Grammar School

Mufasa

Summer . . .
It's cat season
And Mufasa doesn't play about!

He's fast, he's quick,
He's lean, he's mean,
And he's taking his prey *out!*

He stalks,
Like a shadow,
A fly on the wall . . .

He pounces,
Misses
And so he falls

And falls,
And slides,
Behind a chair

And looks
And finds
A peanut there!

But soon,
He does tire,
Of this tasteless treat

And goes
And nibbles,
On his owner's feet.

Summer . . .
Tis the season,
When Mustafa the jungle cat plays about.

Akil Scafe-Smith (12)
Wallington County Grammar School